BOOK II
COUNTRY
Furniture
and
Accessories
with prices

Robert and Harriett Swedberg

Other books by Robert W. and Harriett Swedberg

Off Your Rocker
Victorian Furniture Styles and Prices, Revised
Victorian Furniture Styles and Prices, Book II
Country Pine Furniture Styles and Prices
American Oak Furniture Styles and Prices
Wicker Furniture Styles and Prices
Country Furniture and Accessories with Prices

Cover design by Heather Miller
Cover photograph by Perry L. Struse, Jr.
Location and country furniture
furnished by the
A B C Antique Shoppe
120 - 5th Street
West Des Moines, Iowa

All other photography by the authors
Printing and enlarging by Tom Luse

Library of Congress
Catalog Card Number 82-62062
ISBN 0-87069-376-X

10 9 8 7 6 5 4 3 2 1

Published by

Wallace-Homestead
authoritative books on antiques & collectibles

Wallace-Homestead Book Company
580 Water's Edge Road
Lombard, Illinois 60148

To antique dealers and collectors everywhere . . . those we know and those we want to know.

Acknowledgments

The authors express their deepest appreciation to the dealers and collectors who helped in the compilation of this book by providing facts and prices and by allowing their antiques to be photographed and shown in this book.

ABC Antique Shop
Ruth Ankrom and Linda Cron
West Des Moines, Iowa

Alcorn Antiques
Grace and D. I. Alcorn
Centerville, Indiana

Ann's Antiques
Davenport, Iowa

Antiques et cetera
Dale and Jennie Rylander
Altoona, Illinois

Antiques from the Valley
Henry and Ruth Wargolet .
Ontario, Wisconsin

Antiqueland Mall
Judy Hammond, Betty Lee, Carol Moore,
   Madelyn Poteat
Madison, Alabama

Antiqueland Mall
Anthony and Jennifer Orton
Madison, Alabama

The Antique Scene
Rachel Cattrell
Moline, Illinois

The Antique Scene
Lamont and Lillian Hultgren
Moline, Illinois

The Antique Store of Marietta
Marietta, Georgia

Bittersweet Shop
Mark and Gail Estabrooks
Gaylordsville, Connecticut

Susie Burmann Antiques
Rich and Susie Burmann
Eaton, Ohio

Buttermilk Hill Antiques
Terry Husk
Franklin, Pennsylvania

Larry Carrier, Charles Lohr,
   Bruce Rosenwasser
Rocky's Mall,
Weyers Cave, Virginia

Cat 'N Dogs Antiques
John and Norma Beecher
West Branch, Iowa

Columbia Antique Mall
Chic Antiques
Columbia, South Carolina

Churchmouse
Marilyn Johnson
Port Byron, Illinois

Comus Antiques
Trish and Bill Armstrong
New Market, Maryland

Country Antiques
Helen and Lester Lefstein
Quincy, Illinois

Country Collectibles
Joan W. McCall
Kent, Connecticut

The Country Mouse
Kathy Arpan
Columbia Antique Mall
Columbia, South Carolina

Country Quarters
June Wilson and Linda Evans
Augusta, Georgia

Cubbyhole Antiques
Bev Froeliger
Erie, Illinois

Dancy-Polk House Antiques
Mr. and Mrs. R. E. Anderson
Antiqueland Mall
Madison, Alabama

Delagrange Antiques
George and Susan Delagrange
Jeromesville, Ohio

The Dim Lantern
Arlene Harrington
Franklin, Pennsylvania

The Eschenbachs
Dyer, Indiana

Flossie's Antique Shop
Russell, Kansas

Fonda's Antiques
Ethel Fonda
Bennington, Vermont

Lori Franz, Margaret Largent,
  Gale Rakes
Columbia Antique Mall
Columbia, South Carolina

G. and G. Antiques
Virginia and Betty Gause
Newton, Iowa

Ralph and Virginia Gause

Mr. and Mrs. Edward Gabrys

The Grainery Antiques
Shirley and Syd Waggoner
Fort Wayne, Indiana

Greenwood General Store
Sharon Lord
Greenwood, Indiana

Rock Grice
Columbia Antique Mall
Columbia, South Carolina

Patricia Hayes Antiques
Bittersweet Shop
Gaylordsville, Connecticut

Terry Harper
Bookseller
Rouseville, Pennsylvania

Haygood House Antiques
Watkinsville, Georgia

Hearth Antiques
Susanne Edgerly
Bittersweet Shop
Gaylordsville, Connecticut

The Helpers
Roger and Milly Ratcliff
Newton, Iowa

Marjorie Herman

Hillside Antiques
Estelle Holloway
Frankfort, Illinois

Holmes Antiques
Cornwall Bridge, Connecticut

House of Stuff 'N Things
Anna Figg
Buffalo, Iowa

Housman's Antiques
Jan and Dick Housman
Pleasant Valley, Iowa

Julianne and Jack Keim

Kountry Charm Antiques
Louise Keutzer
Arlington, Illinois

LaMere-Brightview Antiques
Moline, Illinois

Lavine's Lantern
Jim and LuAnn Lavine
Geneseo, Illinois

Lionwood Antiques
Charles W. Hilliard
Bath, Ohio

Main Street Antiques and Art
Louis and Colleen Picek
West Branch, Iowa

Mary Ellyn's
Gordon and Mary Ellyn Jensen

Mockingbird Hill Antiques
Lee and Sara Rhoads
Lisbon, Iowa

Dewey Moore Antiques Ltd.
Georgetown, South Carolina

Nana's Front Room Antiques
Kathleen Constable
New Market, Maryland

Sharon Parein
Cordova, Illinois

Bob and Donna Parrott
Knoxville, Tennessee

Vicky and Greg Pelo
LeClaire, Iowa

Plain and Fancy Antiques
Millie Bark
Franklin, Pennsylvania

Greg and Vicky Powell

Mrs. James Rasmussen

The Red Door
Paul and Nancy Gorzelanski
Millard, Nebraska

Red Pump Antiques
Pat Carson and Fay Gustafson
Gerlaw, Illinois

Red Robin Farm
Dorothy McCune
Marengo, Iowa

Robbie's Antiques
Earle and Betty Robison
Lewisburg, Ohio

Randy and Debbie Robison

Room 102
Marjorie Johnson and Barbara Krause
Richmond, Illinois

Sue and Butch Skiles

Earl Slack Antiques
Earl J. Slack
Bittersweet Shop
Gaylordsville, Connecticut

Small Stuff Antiques
Lesley and Captain Ken Denzin
Metairie, Louisiana

Warren K. Sparks, president
Contractors Steel Corporation
Des Moines, Iowa

Spinning Wheel Antiques
Hazel Hanawalt
Woodland Park, Colorado

Mr. and Mrs. William Thurston

Trunks 'N' Treasures
Mel and Terri Hall
Davenport, Iowa

Bill Van Dell

Victoria's Cottage Antiques
Martha Victoria Boone and
  Jo E. Johnson
Guntersville, Alabama

The Village Shop
Susan Braucher
North Canton, Ohio

Richard Waskow
Michigan City, Indiana

Carolyn Watson
Antiqueland Mall
Madison, Alabama

We Like It Shop
Carol Parlee
West Des Moines, Iowa

Westward Ho Antiques
Antiqueland Mall
Madison, Alabama

The Whimsy
Cecilia Lyday and Claire Burnett
Columbia Antique Mall
Columbia, South Carolina

Bill, Vivian, and Rhonda Yemm

Contents

Preface

When authors travel thousands of miles, as we did, in order to photograph antiques, it brings them into contact with knowledgeable dealers from throughout the United States who are willing to share their expertise. It was apparent that various sections of the country prefer specific periods, styles, or types of antiques, causing prices to vary greatly geographically. Because of that factor, this book lists one price under each antique shown, and names the state where it was photographed. To reiterate — dealers determined the dollar signs designated on the items. Where determined, the condition — painted, refinished, repaired, altered — will be indicated.

As everyone knows, a price book serves only as a general guide to values.

Since this is a country and folk art book, it is pertinent to define these two terms as used by the authors.

Definition of Country

Early furniture with a rustic flavor was frequently made at home by hand out of native woods by non-professionals who tinkered at all trades. Usually, these men had only a few tools and they lacked the training to complete complicated designs. Most of their work had plain, functional lines. If Ma needed something, Pa complied to the best of his ability. He might fashion a yarn winder, a spinning wheel, or knock together a utilitarian cupboard. If a country cabinetmaker resided in the area, he worked on a one-to-one basis. When a customer needed a specific article, he produced what that person requested. He completed each order individually.

Then, along came Eli Whitney and Eli Terry, who helped develop the factory system. In 1798, instead of making one musket at a time, Whitney's workers stamped out identical parts that could be assembled to mass-produce guns. By 1808, Terry designed and developed machines and followed a similar system of using interchangeable parts in clocks so that hundreds could be turned out in a short period of time. Lambert Hitchcock applied this idea to chair making in the 1820s, so not all country-type furniture was made by the individual or home cabinetmaker. The cottage suites of the latter 1800s also were mass-produced. They were painted and stenciled with bright birds, colorful flowers, plumb fruits, or peaceful scenes.

Country decors are relaxed and "user-friendly," for their heritage items possess a functional beauty that is comforting to the eyes and spirit.

In today's micro-chip, plasticized world, many people derive great pleasure from collecting objects that actually show the touch of human hands — the hands that created the piece, and the hands that used and admired it for many years.

Definition of Folk Art

Folk art, a part of America's social heritage, represents the joy of self expression by persons, mainly unknown, who frequently lacked training in the field of art. Folk art objects of the past generally met a need and thus were utilitarian, but some were merely ornamental. Much has a delicacy of line, careful color choices, or a pleasing texture that intrigues collectors, although less attractive examples also have appeal.

Folk art does not have to be hand-crafted. It can be produced by industrial methods.

The desire to be creative is not limited to past generations since individuals continue to carve, fashion pottery, paint, sculpt, spin, weave, design quilts, or enjoy other aesthetic pursuits.

10

Additional Prices

As we traveled taking pictures for this book, we recorded prices on many pieces that we did not photograph. We took no dimensions, nor did we record condition. The following chart gives a general and representative price sampling of country articles from shops and shows that we visited.

Price Chart

Article	Prices Recorded
Betty lamp	$85
Bird roasters	$65 $75
Brass dippers/ladles	$84 $85 $175
Brass footman/quads	$150 $245 $295
Brass skimmers	$55 $60 $135
Burl bowls	$295 $350 $445 $475 $565 $595 $845 $850
Butter prints	
cow	$150 $185 $195 $265
eagle	$145 $225 $250
swan	$100
Buttocks baskets	$80 $125
Camphene lamps	$185 $265
Candle boxes	$48 $78 $145 $175 $225
Candle molds	
four-tube	$38
six-tube	$45
eight-tube	$55
twelve-tube	$85
Checkerboards	$95 $115 $145 $265 $275
Chocolate molds (singles and multiples to three)	$47 $62 $67 $72 $80 $84
mold with forty-five rabbits	$195
mold with forty-five Santas	$225
Coverlets	$265 $350 $365 $425 $485 $525 $850
Cradle	$325
Crimpers	$55 $75

Price Chart

Article	Prices Recorded
Double crusie lamp	$65
Dough tray on legs	$550 $600 $895 $900 $925
Dry sinks	$495 $525 $650 $675 $750
Footwarmers	$110 $135 $165 $195
Frakturs	$55 $115 $175
Gooseneck copper tea kettle	$95 $145 $225 $295
Hog scraper candlesticks with ejector and spur	$85 $95
Hooked rugs	$40 $95 $159 $325 $375
Hutch table	$795 $1,200
Ice cream molds	$28 $35 $39 $40 $44 $55 $65 $70 $85 $110
Maple sugar molds	$175 $185
Pantry boxes	$55 $65 $80
Pierced lanterns	$95 $139 $155
Piggin	$195
Revolving iron trivets	$175 $185 $225
Rope beds	$450 $995
Rush light holders	$250 $325
Samplers	$275 $285 $335 $425 $485 $625 $750
Scouring box	$125
Settle benches	$675 $850
Silhouettes	$85 $165 $170 $210
Spiral candlestick	$295
Trammel	$185
Trivets, brass	$30 $47 $70

1 Hearth and home

Hearth and home . . . what a pleasant sound. It presents a picture of varied-colored flames playfully prancing about and nipping at logs. Pioneer life in the United States centered around the fireplace with its fourfold duties of providing heat, light, and a place to cook food, as well as serving as the focal point around which the family pivoted. This is the romantic aspect.

Broiler, 24″ high, **$195.** Kettle, 7″ diameter, 11″ high, **$65.** Indiana.

It was rough work to cut and haul in the logs to keep the fire going all winter, and it was not an efficient heat source. People could "roast" in front while their backs felt drafts. A cook today would find it an inconvenient, heavy chore to prepare meals by baking, boiling, and roasting food over or near open flames. To moderns, fireplaces are a pleasure (or sometimes a fuel bill saver), not a necessity as in the mid-1800s and before.

Box-type cast iron stoves with lids were produced in the United States in 1642, but they were not a successful innovation. A little over one hundred years later, Benjamin Franklin invented a stove that was built into a wall recess like a fireplace but extended out so that three sides sent forth heat. The potbellied stove was available in the early 1800s. In spite of these improvements, most people continued to use fireplaces for approximately two hundred years after the unsuccessful appearance of the first American stove in 1642. The jumbled appearance of the hearth area resulted because it was multipurpose. Even a common home had a pot for cooking and something to set it on or

Fireback or fire plate, impressed central design, 32" high, **$150.** Iowa.

hang it from to keep it near the flames. A moneyed family had a hearth cluttered with utensils and perhaps a narrow chimney cupboard in which excess equipment could be stored.

The pair of small supports for the logs was frequently referred to as firedogs. Larger, more ornamental forms were called andirons. Later, grates were used, with their raised, basketlike structure formed of iron slats to hold the wood and permit air to circulate to keep the flames healthy.

Firebacks, when used, were metal sheets placed against the back of the chimney opening to protect the wall from the heat. Two smaller pieces often served at the sides. Also called fire plates, the heavy cast iron acted as a reflector to send the heat out from the hearth. Firebacks were created in the eastern part of the country for a few

Bellows, 15" long, 7½" wide, **$45.** Illinois.

years in the early 1800s. Elaborate designs were pressed into damp caster's sand with a carved wooden stamp. Molten iron was poured into the resulting impression to cool and harden. At times, small imperfections show where the silica (sand) melted and pitting resulted. Firebacks are uncommon objects to find.

It was not only wise to preserve a fire, but a matter of pride. At night, the fire was banked, perhaps by covering it with ashes so that it would burn low and keep longer. A wealthy English family might have a decorative brass or copper hood with air holes in it called a *curfew* (meaning cover fire) to place over the heaped ashes to confine sparks safely. This was a nightly ritual; hence, a curfew came to indicate the time to be off the streets and ready for bed.

No matter how this heaping up was accomplished, it was necessary come morning to blow on the ashes to rekindle them. A special apparatus, a bellows, performed this function. The sides could be pumped together to force air through a tube to arouse the flames. If this failed and a neighbor was within reach, it was humiliating but handy to ask for a glowing coal to carry home in a metal container to start the fire. Some say that, for a short period, people could insulate their hands with a thick bed of ashes and tote a lighted coal nestled in it. Tradition says the ashes protected the hands from burns and, in winter, kept them warm as well. Don't feel compelled to test this theory. Burns hurt! When there was more than one hearth in a home, tongs could clench the coals to convey them to start another fire elsewhere.

Plaque on bellows reads: "Made by Funsten Bros. & Co. Largest direct handlers of Raw Furs in the world. St. Louis. U.S.A."

Tinder box, tin, 4″ diameter, 3″ high, **$325.** Pistol-type iron tinder lighter, 8″ long, 4″ high, **$400.** Iowa.

Remember, matches that could be struck anywhere were not developed until 1830. These were expensive and not safe. The tips on these splinters of aspen or pine gave off poisonous phosphorus fumes, which often crippled or killed persons at home or factory workers who made them. The United States government took steps to tax this hazard out of existence, and in 1911 a successful non-poisonous formula was developed. This was well after the era of the necessary hearth. In the days before matches when a fire had to be rekindled, tinder boxes provided aid.

A metal tinder box held a piece of steel and of flint, which is a hard rock. When these two were struck together, a spark resulted and was permitted to fall into the tinder — a dry, easily flammable material. Pieces of charred linen or bits of cotton cloth burned readily and could be used to nurture the spark. From

this small start, a candle packed with the kit was lighted. Afterwards, thin pieces of wood were coaxed to burn until a fire greedily snapped and popped again. The English novelist Charles Dickens (1812–1870) claimed that, with luck, it took about half an hour to light a fire with flint and steel. It required some skill, too.

Products of the blacksmith's art were visible about the hearth. The smithy heated iron to a red, malleable glow on a forge that was kept hot by blasts of air from a hand-operated bellows. With his tongs, he held the heated, softened metal on his anvil as he hammered and shaped household tools or utensils — such as trivets, andirons, hinges, latches, roasters, toasters — or completed his main chore of shoeing horses. The blacksmith repaired objects also and was a skilled, essential citizen in the community. The fireplace pictured features some of his products. Notice the variety of holders. An American copper teakettle has a spout that resembles a goose's neck and is therefore referred to as a gooseneck spout. Its sides and base are dovetailed together, similar to the interlocking of jigsaw puzzle pieces or lacing the fingers of both hands together. The dovetail joint acquired its name because it vaguely resembles that bird's tail. The kettle fits into a convenient hanging device called an idle back that permits it to be tilted without being removed from its smithy-made support. Ingenious, convenient devices such as this were developed to aid the cook and increase efficiency.

Various holders suspended pots and kettles over the fire. An adjustable version was a hook arrangement called a trammel. It could be shortened or lengthened, depending on the height of the flames that exuded different degrees of heat and to accommodate cooking containers of various sizes that hung from it. Often a pan had a built-in holder on the handle and swiveled on the hook.

The iron kettle shown on the S hook is signed "S.A." It could have been initialed by a man proud of the quality of his work, or is possibly the identification mark of the owner. Its round body appears to be pieced together, and it has a brass knob on the lid. Another trammel holds an iron kettle with a rounded bottom that permits the flames to curl up around its sides. The three legs allow it to sit on the hearth floor. A baby food kettle with tiny feet dan-

Fireplace interior from left to right: American copper gooseneck teakettle, 7″ diameter, 13″ high, **$285.** Idle back on which the kettle rests, **$210.** Sawtooth trammel, **$125,** holding fireplace pan with built-in hook, 11″ diameter, 13½″ high, **$85.** Kettle on S-hook, 7″ diameter, 11″ high, **$250.** Iron kettle, three legs, 11½″ diameter, 18″ high, **$125.** Baby food kettle, 6½″ diameter, 8″ high, not priced. Iowa.

gles from a hook on a trammel chain. It traveled to the state of Iowa in a covered wagon, and its dealer-owner has never seen another one.

Examine the next photograph. Notice that candle holders could have prongs so that they could be stuck in beams to shed their light. The one on the right also could be hung over a chair rail. Moving from left to right, tongs were helpful when burning logs had to be shifted about. The iron skimmer has embossed (raised) decorations on the handle. The revolving hand-wrought broiler was set over coals so that a slice of meat could be turned as it cooked. Sometimes, a low pan was placed underneath to catch the dripping juices. The dipper, with ornamented handle, matches the skimmer to form a set. The toaster could face the fire; some had rotating heads.

The trivet (stand with three legs) to the rear in the photograph includes a prong that slides back and forth. It was positioned to support the handle of the pan that was placed on the sliding handle rest, and it was adjusted as necessary. The revolving trivet in front held pots close to the fire or over the coals.

The blacksmith who hammered out the andirons created attractive, reverse-turn ends and rounded feet termed "penny feet" because of their shape. Although the andirons are shown as a pair, they differ from each other. The left one is several inches longer and higher than the one to the right. The smithy gauged his work by sight instead of actual measurement.

Iron was not the only metal present in the chimney area. Here is how one brass utensil evolved. Meat roasting

Fireplace tools from left to right: Iron tongs, 20″ long, **$120.** Iron skimmer with embossed handle, 18½″ long, **$82.50.** Revolving meat broiler, **$225.** Dipper, iron, with embossed handle, 19″ long, **$82.50.** Toaster, 13¼″ wide, 14″ long, **$250.** Iowa.

18

Hanging utensils from left to right: tongs, 20″ long, **$120**. Copper pan, 7½″ diameter, 16½″ long, **$145**. Copper pan, 5″ diameter, 11½″ long, **$145**. Brass skimmer, 5″ diameter, 19½″ long, **$120**. Brass, rat-tail ladle, 5″ diameter, 20″ long, **$95**. Copper pan with iron handle, signed "E . . . D.H. made in N.Y.," 4¼″ diameter, 9½″ long, **$145**. Dipper, brass, 20½″ long, **$95**. Iowa.

over a fire requires turning to prevent it from burning. Spits rotated by hand were utilized, but Mary Earle Gould in her book *Antique Tin and Tole Ware* sketches a word picture of children twisting a cord that supported a meat-filled spit. When released, it unwound, rotating the meat so it cooked evenly. Other sources tell about "spit hounds," small dogs that were bred and trained to trot on tread mills to activate spits. Eventually, a device vaguely resembling a bottle was developed. It was referred to as a bottle jack. After its spring-operated mechanism was wound, it rotated slowly. Commonly made of brass, these jacks were popular in the 1800s and are available currently.

It is unusual to secure a matching set of kitchen utensils. Frequently, the brass pancake turner is missing, but four pieces marked "F.B.S. Canton, O. Pat. Jan. 28, '86" have remained together. A skimmer, a two-tine fork, and a dipper complete the foursome in the picture. Although these are of the late 1800s, similar equipment served housewives who cooked over an open hearth.

Copper utensils abounded and frequently were made of thick, heavy metal. The interlocking joining (dovetails) can be seen on the bottom of the first two pans on the left in the next photo. The skimmer is signed with "OG" on the handle while the ladle handle terminates in a thin line where it is fastened to the bowl. Someone in the past thought such construction resembled a rat's tail and the name remained. It forms a rat-tail handle. The little pan's iron handle is marked, but part is no longer distinct. It reads "E...D.H. made in N.Y." It is an unusually small size that is hard to find. A copper dipper was a cook's aid also.

Wrought iron, penny-foot andirons, 12″ to 14″ long, 12½″ to 14″ high, **$55** a pair. Indiana.

A word of caution: old copper and brass articles can have harmful ingredients in them and should not be employed in cooking unless they have a good lining of a non-toxic metal such as tin. Some pottery, especially when unglazed, may present problems also, and lead is dangerous. The advisability of using certain types of well-worn plated silver is questionable. Furthermore, nickel-silver tableware contains no silver but is an alloy of nickel, copper, and zinc. When its nickel-plated surface is thin, it can cause illness. There are passé objects that are better to look at or to decorate with than to associate with food because they can be health hazards.

Since pots, pans, and kettles were prevalent on the hearth, stands that kept them near or over the heat were present also. When these had three legs, they were called trivets. Purists maintain that a four-legged type is rightfully a "quad" (or, in England, a "footman") because trivet connotes three and quad indicates four. Certain types included a hanging feature that attached to the grate to hold the pot near the flames.

A chestnut roaster was a fun item to have hanging around. The brass or copper container with its perforated top prevented the nuts from escaping as they heated. Since there was a long handle, a person could hold the roaster over the fire and remain a safe distance away.

A metal box with a long shaft that resembled the chestnut roaster was a bed warmer. On cold nights it was filled with coals and carried to the bedchambers because they usually were not heated. After it was moved back and forth under the covers, occupants were able to climb into a warmed bed.

Brass rotisserie, called a bottle jack, 4¼″ diameter, 14″ high, **$185.** Ohio.

Brass kitchen implement set, marked "F.B.S. Canton, O. Pat. Jan. 28, '86": skimmer, two-tine fork, dipper, pancake turner, 14″ to 19″ long, **$450** the set. Illinois.

Tin was less expensive and more readily available for the family of ordinary means to own; thus, the tinsmith's products were in evidence on the hearth. Peddlers acquired their wares and traversed the country. Some had packs on their backs, others mounted on horseback, but some had horse-drawn covered wagons equipped with built-in shelves to store combs, needles, boxes, dishpans, pots, pins, pitchers, scissors, trays, and other articles. It was exciting when the tin peddler came to a remote farm bringing news from the outside world. If he told stories well or could sing, his visit was anticipated greatly. The housewife saved clean rags, wood ashes, tallow, and fats to trade for his merchandise; and the two enjoyed the bartering game. The woman got her pots, and the peddler would sell the ashes and fats to soap makers. Linen rags became paper, and tallow turned into candles.

Brass quad trivet, called a "footman" in England, 5″ deep, 9″ long, 5½″ high, **$95.** Connecticut.

Wrought iron revolving trivet in foreground, 10½″ diameter, 21¼″ long, **$65.** Trivet in background with sliding rest for pan handle, 9″ diameter, 21″ long, handle rest 14″ high, **$175.** Ohio.

Brass trivet, wooden handle, 5″ wide, 14″ long, **$125.** Iowa.

Copper teakettle and fireplace stand that hangs on grate, **$210** both pieces. Pennsylvania.

Chestnut roaster, 12″ diameter, 43″ long, **$76.** Hand-forged fork, 35″ long, **$82.** Ohio.

Tin bird roaster, 11½″ wide, 4″ deep, 9″ high, **$185.** Iowa.

A tin bird roaster held small fowl close to the fire. Quail, also known as bob white because their call sounds like "bob, bobwhite," are currently a gourmet's delight. In fireplace days, the plucked and cleaned bird was hooked securely in a small reflector-type oven that had narrow sides. This was set near the fire. As the cooking proceeded, the juicy drippings were caught in the base and contained in its turned-up edges. Similar small ovens met other needs.

A special fish cooker was made of punched tin. In order to pierce a piece of tin, it was placed over a board. Holes were made by hammering a nail through it with irregular results. Sometimes, a strainer-type object such as this was inserted in the base of an elongated pan that was used to roast fish.

Fish cooker with perforated drainage holes, 19″ long, **$175.** Indiana.

Wooden framed footwarmer has tin chamber with two punched hearts on front and back, 9″ wide, 8″ deep, 5½″ high, **$185.** Iowa.

Footwarmers left to right: wooden case with punched diamond designs, metal insert pan, 9½″ wide, 7″ deep, 6″ high, **$165.** Wooden case with turned posts, tin chamber, 13½″ wide, 10″ deep, 7½″ high, **$185.** Wooden frame supporting punched tin chamber, 8″ wide, 8″ deep, 6½″ high, **$165.** Iowa.

Tin footwarmer has tiny punched hearts, 10″ diameter, 6″ high, **$225.** Iowa.

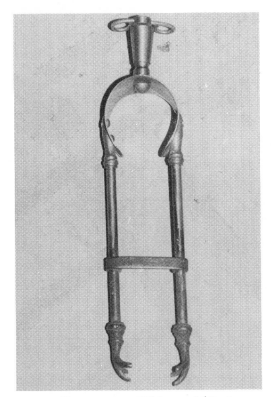

Iron and brass tongs, 12″ long, **$45.** Iowa.

Brass trivet with iron legs, wooden handle, circa 1930, **$65.** Indiana.

Iron firebacks: two side pieces, 15¼″ wide, 30″ high, **$125** each. Ohio.

Bellows, Irish origin, operated by turning wheel that activated a series of fans within wooden housing; air was brought in through the side vents and expelled through the nozzle. Made from eighteenth century to 1920; 7½″ wide, 7½″ high, 23″ long, **$400.** Ohio.

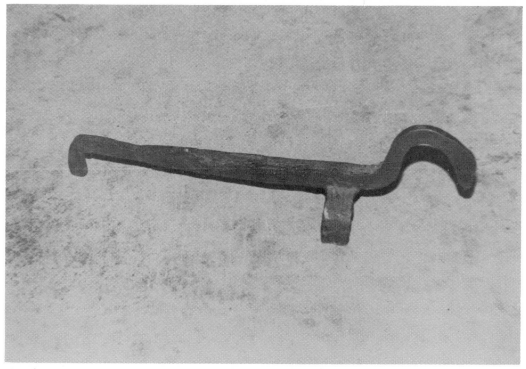

Fireplace rest made by a blacksmith, 18″ long, **$25.** South Carolina.

Fireplace setting: copper candy pan, 20″ handle to handle, 7″ deep, **$250.** Chain trammel, **$180.** Black kettle marked Marietta, Pa. **$65.** Skillet, 12″ diameter, 45″ long, **$185.** Indiana.

Wrought iron roaster, 23″ long, 12″ wide, 12″ deep, **$175.** Connecticut.

Three-footed iron saucepan, 6¼″ diameter, 5″ high, 16¼″ long, **$85.** Stand or rest, 7″ diameter, 4″ high, **$55.** Iowa.

Wrought iron tilting American broiler, New England origin, 14¾″ diameter, **$450.** Ohio.

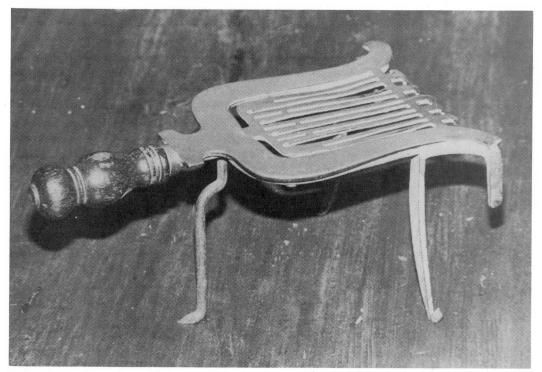

Brass trivet, Australian origin, 11½″ long, 6½″ wide, 5″ high, **$75.** Connecticut.

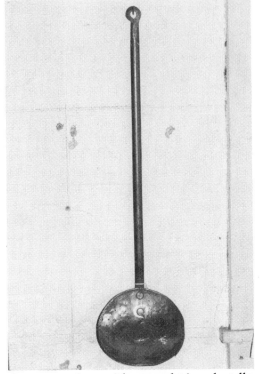

Dipper, 11½″ diameter, 43″ long, **$76.**
Strainer, 11″ diameter, 42½″ long, **$76.**
Ohio.

Copper strainer with wrought iron handle,
7″ diameter, 26½″ long, **$115.** Indiana.

Brass kitchen utensils with iron handles, left to right: dipper, 21½″ long, **$70.** Dipper, 19½″
long, **$60.** Skimmer, late 1700s, 19″ long, **$95.** Dipper, 18″ long, **$55.** Dipper, 18″ long,
$60. Illinois.

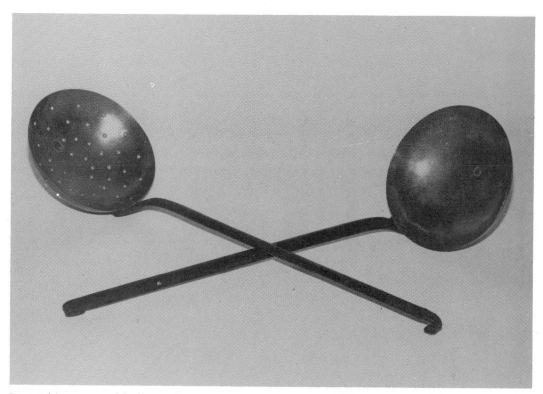

Brass skimmer and ladle with iron handles, 17″ long, **$95** each. Illinois.

Copper saucepan, 5½″ diameter, 6″ high, handle 5¾″ long, **$65.** Ohio.

Copper pans, iron handles, dovetailed bottom on left pan, 7¾″ diameter, 4¼″ high, handle 9¼″ long, **$196.** Capped bottom on right pan, 8½″ diameter, 5″ high, handle 8″ long, signed "R," **$210.** Iowa.

Zinc-lined copper pan, signed "H. & M. Co., N.Y." is 12″ in diameter, 8″ high, handle 13″ long, **$340.** Iowa.

Brass scoop, 8″ long, **$30.** Copper chafing pan, name on bottom reads "Charles Hauck & Sons, Brooklyn, N.Y.," 8½″ diameter, 2″ high, **$40.** Illinois.

Brass, double boiler, dovetail bottom, 9″ diameter, 5¾″ high, insert 4½″ high, **$125.** Illinois.

Copper four-piece candy making set; bottom pan 22″ diameter, 10½″ high; insert pan 19½″ diameter, 9½″ high; five-hole dipper, 14″ long. Set, **$670.** Iowa.

Copper bucket, dovetailed bottom and side, eighteenth century, 8½″ diameter, 5¼″ high, replaced handle, **$165.** Illinois.

Rolled-edge copper kettle, 26″ diameter, 18″ high, **$325.** Illinois.

Spun brass jelly kettle, 9″ diameter, 4¼″ high, **$125.** Iowa.

Copper kettle with capped bottom, rolled edge, was made in Minnesota, signed "Olsen," 24″ diameter, 12″ high, **$375.** Iowa.

Copper pitcher, dovetailed 4″ from base, origin Pella, Iowa, 5¾″ diameter, 11½″ high, **$200.** Iowa.

Brass teakettle, 5″ diameter, 8″ high, **$80.** Ohio.

Copper gooseneck teakettles, 10½″ high, **$95** each. Cast iron, wood-burning stove, 20″ wide, 12″ deep, 20″ high, **$155.** Illinois.

Copper teakettle, 5″ diameter, 5″ high, **$55.**
Ohio.

Copper teakettle, patented 1876, rolled edges, 10¼″ diameter, 13″ high with handle up, **$235.**
Illinois.

Perhaps the most religious fireplace article was the portable foot stove or foot warmer that held hot coals. In the North, when winter winds began to blow, horses pulled sleighs across snow-filled roads. On the long ride to church, a girl didn't pout when a brother crushed her full skirt, and boys didn't bicker. Instead, children huddled close together under thick robes to keep away the chill while warmers toasted their toes. At church, people sat with their feet on the small stoves as they listened to the long sermons. If services lasted all day, more coals were added during the noon break when families ate the food they had brought. A hot baked potato held in the hand was an edible heater. As structures, churches and meetinghouses were not the warmest places to sit for hours at a time. Members of the congregation had to develop their own methods of dealing with the cold.

It's no wonder the fireplace was cluttered. It met so many needs . . . heating, cooking, lighting, socializing, and providing hot coals for bed and foot warmers. The hearth and home were indeed a union.

Copper coffeepot, chained lid, scorched wooden handle, 10″ diameter, 13½″ high, **$125.** Iowa.

2 Metals

Metals found in the earth include copper, tin, lead, silver, zinc, gold, and iron. These are natural. Man-made combinations are referred to as alloys. Chief among them are brass, bronze, and pewter. Frequently, these mixtures were made to provide greater strength, retard rust, or fill special needs. Nature's copper tends to be reddish pink or golden pink. Brass is a golden yellow alloy of copper, zinc, and sometimes tin. Bronze, chiefly composed of copper and tin, tends to be reddish-brown in hue. Verdigris is an uneven green or greenish-blue, rustlike film that develops on copper, brass, and bronze, usually after they have been exposed to moist air for a considerable period of time. A magnet applied to these metals will not adhere but slides off immediately. An exception would be a base of a lamp, vase, or candlestick that had been weighted inside with some other metal. In that case, the magnet could cling to this specific area. Many metal objects performed useful functions in the home, while others were decorative. Brass, copper, and bronze items are compatible with almost any decor from casual country to the most formal settings. They can add an elite touch to home environments

Brass jardiniere or planter, dovetail on sides, 10¼″ diameter, 8½″ high, **$185.** Iowa.

The French word for tin is tole. Therefore, this term includes all objects fashioned from this metal, plain or decorated. Some people, however, feel that toleware refers only to painted tin products. The Chinese and Japanese were skilled in ornamental techniques. The Orientals secured resin from a certain native tree as a base for their quick-drying lacquer and built it up in layers on objects, frequently after artificial color was added. Their centuries-old art produced a polished, hard, shiny surface, which they decorated in various ways, often in relief (raised above the surface). The English called this Oriental lacquer work "japanning." They tried to copy it, but did not use built-up layers of lacquer as the Japanese and Chinese did. Instead, they achieved the shiny, brownish-black effect by applying mineral asphalt in varnish over tin. Af-

Tin wall case with mirror, 10″ diameter, **$30.** Iowa.

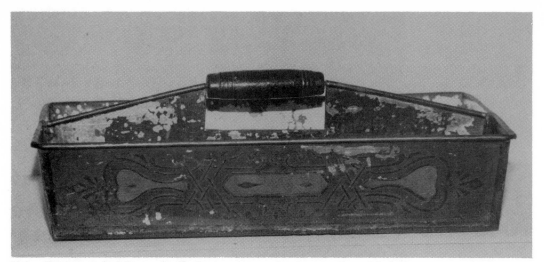

Tole silverware holder or knife box, maroon background, gold design, circa 1850, 13½" wide, 9" deep, 4½" high, **$65.** Iowa.

terwards, the treated object was placed in a drying oven to harden. This asphaltum coating somewhat resembled the Oriental work.

Tin products could be enhanced further with painted-on freehand drawings or by the use of stencils. A cutout design was placed over the object, and paint or bronze was dabbed in the openings to form the decoration. Such stencils have aided artists for centuries.

Not many tin products were made in this country until after the Revolutionary War (1775–1783) for two reasons. Natural tin was not available along the Atlantic coast where the settlements were, and the English wanted their colonists to import manufactured articles from them, not produce their own. Partly because of this, pre-1800 examples are rare, but by 1820–1830, stenciling and freehand painting were being done in the United States. New England tinsmiths were inspired to show vividly colored native fruits and flowers in elaborate variations on their trays, canisters, boxes, teapots, jugs, coffeepots, or sugar bowls. Pennsylvania artists chose to depict geometric designs, birds, pomegranates, horses,

people, angels, and tulips in bright array. Peacocks proved to be popular. Fancy scenes with churches, houses, villages, and castles might have been inspired by imported tin products from England.

Prominent colors were vibrant red, yellow, green, and blue against red or brownish-black backgrounds. Besides its attractive qualities, painting had another purpose. It protected the surface from rust. Generally speaking, japanned ware eventually came to mean any such painted metalware. Peddlers on foot, horseback, or driving carts were the distributors of tin products from about 1830 through the Civil War (1861–1865) when railroads helped put these traveling merchants out of business.

Novices should be aware that their toleware should not be handled continously. The old decorations do wear off. Most collectors would warn beginners not to retouch or repaint old toleware. Don't cover metal objects with black paint—it's a primary rule. This decreases their value. Truly old examples generally have small age checks across the painted surfaces, and colors of the past are different from the new

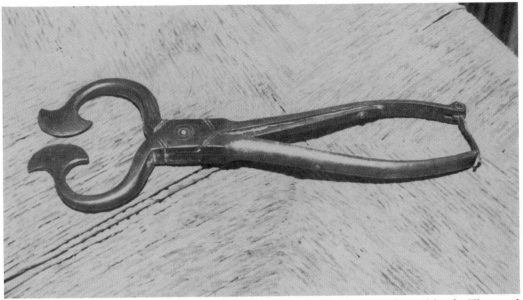

Sugar nippers or cutters, **$120.** Sugar once came in a hard, cone-shaped loaf. The cook hit it with a sugar hammer to break pieces off. Then these pieces were nipped with the cutter to make the lumps smaller. Connecticut.

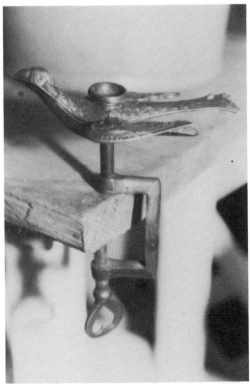

Brass sewing bird, marked "Feb. 15, 1853." Some were made of wood or iron and attached to the worktable. Pressure on the bird's tail would open and close the beak to hold the fabric, **$95.** Connecticut.

Copper ice cream cone with nickel top and brass holder, 13″ high, **$170.** It hung in candy stores or over the soda fountains in drugstores to advertise the five-cent cone. Illinois.

Brass mortar and pestle used by housewives, doctors, and druggists to grind spices or medicines, 5¼″ diameter, 5½″ high. Pestle, 9½″ high, **$150.** Ohio.

Miniature brass mortar and pestles, 2″ high, **$27.50;** 1½″ high, **$25;** 1″ high, **$22.** Illinois.

Brass sadiron stands, usually called trivets. Stand at left has heart motif; trivet in center has date of 1894; and stars form the design of the third. Each 8″ long, **$55** each. Illinois.

Brass watering can with two handles for tipping and carrying, 12″ high, **$115.** Illinois.

Brass spittoon or cuspidor, widely used when tobacco chewing was prevalent, 7½″ diameter, 8″ high, **$45.** Ohio.

hues. Another sign of recent manufacture is heavily applied paint. Expect very old tin items to show the irregularities of work done by hand. Today, much tinware is fashioned from thin sheets of iron coated with tin.

Tin bathtub, stenciled, red rim, green body, 33″ wide, 16½″ deep, 10″ high, **$58.** Iowa.

Tole hanging candle box with hinged lid, painted red, 10″ wide, 4½″ deep, **$195.** Iowa.

Tole document box, handcrafted, brass handle, eighteenth century, 8″ wide, 4″ deep, 4″ high, **$625.** Pennsylvania.

Chicken scale; head projected through small end of funnel as it was weighed. Scale diameter 10″, funnel 12½″ long, **$50.** Iowa.

Sausage stuffer, tin body, brass band. At butchering time the sausage gun was filled with chopped pork and spices, then pumped into the intestine skin that was drawn over the nozzle. The resulting rings of sausage were stored for future use. 5″ diameter, 21½″ long, **$55.** Ohio.

Tin coffeepot with cup sitting in top (probably a later addition), origin Pennsylvania, circa 1850, 11½" high. **$95.** Illinois.

Tin wall pocket with scalloped edges, punched design, dated 1872, 15½" wide, 3¼" deep, 19" high, **$125.** Iowa.

Tin coffeepot, 10" high, **$55.** Illinois.

Tin utensils from left to right: muffineer (held sugar or cinnamon to be sprinkled over muffins), 4½ ″ high, **$35.** Tea flask, 6″ high, **$25.** Child's kettle, 5″ diameter, **$25.** Connecticut.

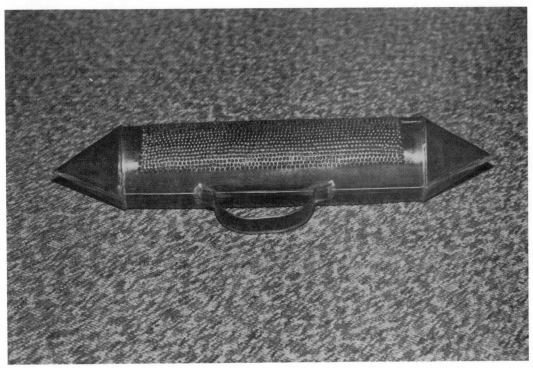

Tin grater with handle, 15″ long, **$65.** Iowa.

Buggy whip holder, 16″ diameter, **$50.** Ohio.

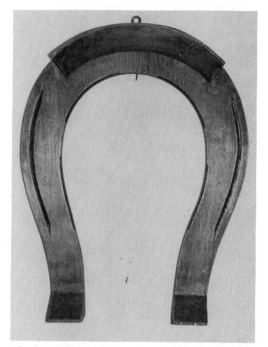

Blacksmith's wooden horseshoe sign, late nineteenth century, 17″ wide, 21″ high, **$165.** Iowa.

Iron match holder and striker, marked "Pat. Jan. 15, 1867." The first American patent for matches was registered in 1836. Measures 3½″ wide, 6″ high, **$55.** Iowa.

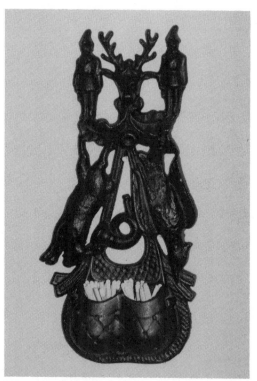

Iron match holder depicts hunting scene with men and game, 5″ wide, 11″ high, **$75.** Iowa.

Years ago, many lamps, lanterns, candleholders, and other lighting devices were made of tin. Examples can be seen in chapter four.

Colonists started a blast furnace soon after they settled in Jamestown, Virginia, but an Indian attack caused it to be abandoned in 1622. The first continuing ironworks in the United States was established in 1646 at Lynn, Massachusetts (now Saugus). This metal is versatile. Wrought iron can be forged (shaped with blows or pressure from a hammer, press, or other machinery). It can be welded, which means it is heated so that it can be fused (joined by melting), hammered, or pressed together. It is tough and resists corrosion. It is ductile since it can be drawn into thin wires or hammered thin. Cast iron cannot be forged or welded. It is hard, brittle, and readily fusible. The molten iron is poured into molds to solidify into shape. (There is an exception. A certain type of cast iron is malleable.)

The role of the town smithy (blacksmith) was described previously because he wrought by hand much needed fireplace equipment, utensils, and essential farm implements. The blacksmith shoed the horses and kept transportation running, much as the iron and steel industry does today producing metals needed in cars, trucks, buses, ships, planes, or trains. Now, tractors and trucks serve human beings; but until the early 1900s, the horse plowed the fields, hauled hay, and was the general beast of burden. Therefore, the blacksmith's work was important as he heated and pounded into shape the required iron objects or mended broken ones.

Iron and steel (an alloy made from iron and other materials) are the most economical and useful metals known. A tiny pin, huge machines that turn out necessary products, or a towering building owe their existence to knowledge acquired about these metals. Today, steel nails turned out by machines are so common that bent ones carelessly are tossed away. Conversely, pioneers, who had to tediously shape their own nails or purchase them from blacksmiths, considered them precious.

Iron coffee grinder fastens to vertical surface, hinged handle can fold in. Grinder is marked: "Mft. by, A. J. and Geo W. M. Vandecrift, Guilford, Conn., May 17, 1878 Pat." Owner says this one was used on a prairie schooner in the late 1800s, 8″ wide, 10″ high, **$115.** Iowa.

Corn grinder, Letz Mfg. Co., painted green, used to make cornmeal, 16″ diameter, 16″ high, **$75.** Kentucky.

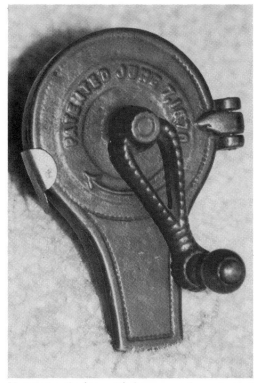

Iron meat hook, held sides of butchered meat, 12″ wide, 13″ high, **$30.** Connecticut.

Nutmeg grinder with brass catch, patented June 7, 1870, 4″ high, **$135.** Ohio.

Open view of nutmeg grinder.

Wrought iron dough scraper was used to scrape out doughboxes or large bowls, 3½″ wide, **$85.** Ohio.

Steel Grass Strippe used to collect seeds (often called headers) 12″ wide, 11″ deep, 18″ high, **$95.** Iowa.

Iron star, used in pairs as a structural support in early homes. A star at each end of the house was attached to an iron rod to keep the walls from leaning, 9½″ wide, **$75.** Ohio.

Leg irons of the Civil War era, 3″ diameter, $125. Iowa.

Pot metal doorstop, 9″ wide, 3″ deep, 8″ high, $65. Ohio.

Holder for cigarettes, cigars, matches, made of pot metal with brass inserts, 8″ wide, 5½″ high, $175. Iowa.

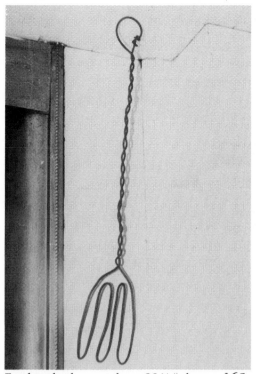

Feather bed smoother, 23¼" long, **$65.**
Pennsylvania.

Iron doorstop, 10" wide, 9½" high, **$60.** Illinois.

3 Treenware

Put an "n" on the end of tree, and the word treen results, the old plural of tree. This is an archaic name for woodenware, which could range in size usually from a small flax spinning wheel down to the tiniest boxes. Many treenware objects were employed in the preparation of food, and much was fashioned at home by hand, to meet a need. When a housewife needed a mortar and pestle to pulverize hunks of spices, garden herbs, or pieces of hard sugar cones, her husband made her one. If he was not too skillful and lacked tools, he might hack off a piece of hollow log, smooth it slightly inside, and flatten its base so it would sit on a table. This would be the bowl (mortar). A heavy, fat stick, rounded at the bottom end and narrowed to form a hand grip at the top could serve as a pestle or pounder. Ma's tool was done.

Mortar and pestle set has 7½"-high pestle and 8"-high mortar, **$75.** Maryland.

Another man might burn and scrape out the inside of a piece of log until it was even, shape the outside slightly, and incise (cut in) some decorative lines. He would fashion the pestle with a wide base and a narrow handle that would fit easily into a feminine hand. As a result of his careful work, his wife's mortar and pestle were both functional and attractive.

Special woods sometimes were formed into distinctive tools. Have you ever seen a tree with a hump back or a wart-like growth? That abnormal section has an attractive mottled or speckled pattern when cut and is called burl. Thin slices of it were glued to drawers, door panels, or tops of furniture as ornamental veneers.

In America, ash, maple, and walnut trees are the most common sources for this wood with the wild grain, and mortars could be formed from a piece of the hump. Because burl articles are not common and have a beauty of their

Mortar and pestle (left) with 7¾"-high mortar painted red, **$95.** Mortar and pestle (right) has 6½"-high mortar, burl wood, **$350.** Iowa.

Mortar and pestle set, 6"-high pestle, 3¾"-high burl mortar, **$175.** Connecticut.

Burl bowls and burl dippers: (upper left) bowl 9" diameter, **$250.** Dipper, 9" long, **$65.** (Upper right) bowl, 11" diameter, **$600.** Dipper, 13" long, **$85.** (Lower left) bowl, 7" diameter, **$250.** (Lower right) bowl, 3½" diameter, **$85.** Iowa.

Cottage cheese bowl with drainage hole in bottom, 6¾″ diameter, 6½″ high, **$55**. Iowa.

At times, a hole was made in the bottom of a bowl for a reason. Cottage cheese, the simplest, easiest kind of cheese to prepare, was made in various ways. Curds are the coagulated part of milk that forms when it sours. The whey is the watery portion. The two are separated either by straining off the curds or by draining out the whey. When the curds were stirred or squeezed with a paddle or spoon in the bowl shown, the agitation caused the excess liquid to flow out, leaving behind the soft, white lumps. These would be salted and otherwise seasoned according to the taste of the cheese maker, but no curing was necessary. The product could be eaten immediately.

In another process, the curds were placed in a cloth bag, and the whey was squeezed out as much as possible. The curds in the bag were then hung up to drip dry before the cottage cheese was eaten.

The Georgia cheese drainer was scooped out from a piece of a log. The leg under the spout is shorter than the two at the back. Milk or cream could be soured with rennet, which came from the membrane lining or contents of the fourth stomach of an unweaned calf. When the sour milk was poured into this slanted wooden bowl, stirred and agitated, the whey would drain off into a bucket beneath the spout. Paddles were constructed so that they could press down on the curd mass that had to be cut at intervals with a wooden curd knife to separate it so it could be worked. Afterward, the coagulated lumps would be packed along the sides to allow more of the liquid to run out into the ditch left in between into a bucket beneath. The matted curds were turned over to dry more thoroughly. They were cut and broken apart, mixed, salted, and other flavoring ingredients were added as desired.

own, their price is higher than that of similar, ordinary wooden articles.

Burl bowls, too, have a distinctive mottled grain. They were containers used for required tasks such as chopping vegetables, mincing fruits, or mixing pastry.

Ladles, dippers, and butter paddles also could have this pronounced burl pattern.

Mixing bowls, which were constantly in use in the kitchen area, can have nicks in them where the blade of a chopper made contact, or scrape marks may be present where spoons daily battered the wood. Frequently, a frugal housewife did not toss out a favorite bowl because it split. It could be pulled together by a leather thong laced through holes drilled on either side of the crack. Thus, it was recycled for additional years of service. One dealer who found a similar mend removed the thong and patched the holes. To her consternation, she later read about such mends. She pulled out her plugs and returned the bowl to the condition in which she found it.

Burl bowl and burl dippers: bowl has uneven diameter of 9½″ to 12″, **$245.** (Left) dipper signed "J. W. Trudell, 1874" is 16″ long, 3½″ diameter bowl, **$145.** (Right) early 1800s dipper, 11½″ long, 3¾″ bowl diameter, **$70.** Illinois.

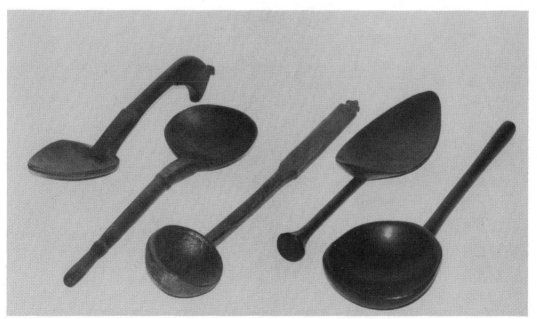

Kitchen treenware from left to right: butter worker with figural handle, 8″ long, **$45.** Ladle with "K X" initials, 8½″ long, bowl 3″ diameter, **$35.** Dipper, 11½″ long, bowl 2½″ diameter, **$47.50.** Spoon, 8¼″ long, **$29.** Spoon, stained by berries, 10¼″ long, bowl 3″ diameter, **$32.** Illinois.

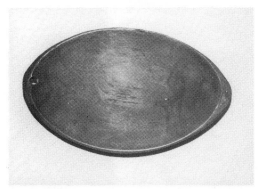

Chopping bowl, 22″ long, 13″ wide, 4″ high, origin Maine, circa 1850, **$125.** Pennsylvania.

Then, they were pressed into blocks or rounds to remove more moisture. These were cured for two weeks or more, depending on the type of cheese sought. Aging could take a year or more. A smooth, mild cheese required less curing time than a stronger flavored, drier product. Some types also went through a heating process.

In another method, the curds were placed in a slatted, circular or square drainer that had a cheesecloth liner. A rack supporting the drainer was called a cheese ladder. This was placed over a tub to catch the whey that was saved to "slop" (feed) the hogs. Later, the cheese, encased in a cloth, would be hung to dry more thoroughly. The hardened mass would be cut with a cheese knife, and the broken up parts would go into a bowl to be salted and worked with a paddle to reduce the amount of whey. Herbs or seasoning were added. Afterward, a cheese press with a screwing device squeezed out any remaining

Batter jug, Albany glaze, **$110.** Miscellaneous spoons, **$3.50** to **$5** each. Illinois.

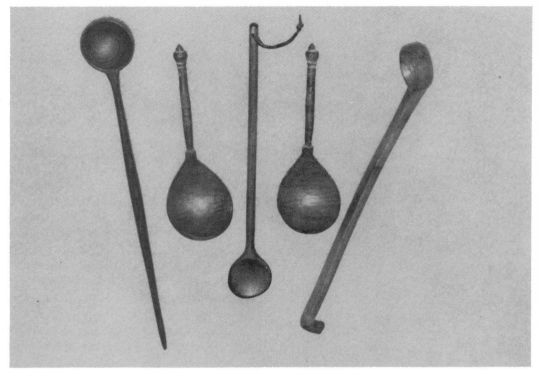

Treenware from left to right: 12″ taster, **$42.** Tiger maple scoop or measure, 7″ long, **$38.** Taster, 11″ long, **$42.** Scoop or measure in tiger maple, 7″ long, **$38.** Taster, 13½″ long, **$42.** Ohio.

Mixing bowl, 24″ long, 15″ wide, 5″ high, **$95.** Jacquard coverlet in background, **$550.** Indiana.

Ash burl wood bowl, 13″ diameter, 4½″ high, **$400.** Indiana.

Cheese press-drainer, 26″ long, 10½″ wide, height varies from 16″ to 15″ at drain end to permit liquid to escape, **$65.** Georgia.

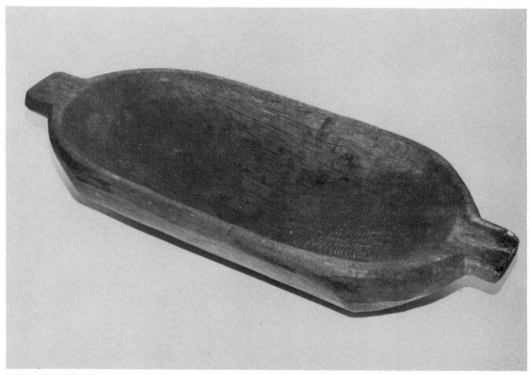

Butter or cheese making bowl, 22″ long, 9½″ wide, 4½″ deep, with pouring spout, **$75.** Illinois.

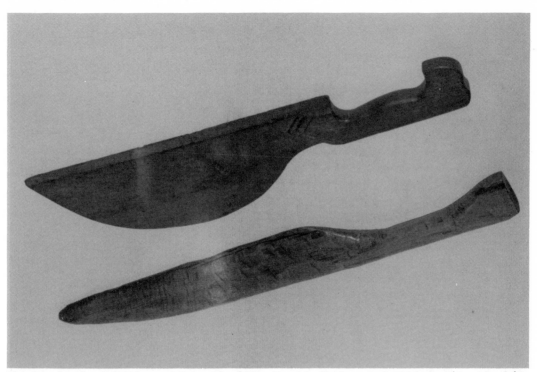

Flax breaker (top) 19″ long, 2½″ wide, **$39.** Curd knife (bottom) 17″ long, 4″ wide, **$49.** Iowa.

liquid. In some cases, the top and bottom of the cheese were buttered daily for two weeks before being stored away in a special cupboard where flies couldn't contaminate it. This is a simplified description of a process that consumed a great deal of personal effort, encompassing many days, in an era before cheese making became a commercial venture.

It was not until 1856 that a large quantity of butter was produced by a professional creamery. After that, this farm industry started to move from the home to the factory. Also in 1856, a cream separator was developed. Before that time, it took eighteen to twenty-four hours for the cream, which was lighter in weight, to rise to the top of the milk so that it could be skimmed off. Churns with cream in them were swung, rocked, shaken, or a dasher was plunged up and down in them. Boys might be assigned to keep them moving. Goats,

Butter churn, wooden staves, 22″ high, 9″ diameter at top, **$225.** Illinois.

Butter carrier in which farmers shipped butter to customers, 19½" wide, 17" deep, 17" high, **$95.** Connecticut.

sheep, or dogs on treadmills powered some large churns and cream separators, but women considered it their task to make butter. (Traditionally, the farm wives received the money from the sale of butter and eggs.) When cream was agitated vigorously, the fat in the cream became solidified. The remaining fat-free liquid, called buttermilk, was drained off. Then the butter was washed in cold water, worked to remove liquid and to mix in salt, and finally molded into shape.

A retired farmer stated that he found it soothing to work butter back in the days when he and his wife were on the farm. The man sat down, and a large bowl with a pouring spout at one end was placed in his lap. He held a butter worker (a paddle) in his hand, and repeatedly pushed against the mass, pulling it toward his body. This action squeezed out the liquid, which drained into a bucket that stood under the spout and near the farmer's feet.

Treenware, left to right: butter dish, 6" diameter, would have had glass dish in it, **$60.** Mortar and pestle, **$69.** Funnel, 6½" high, **$65.** Iowa.

Other people operated special butter workers. These were wooden frames with a roller attachment that did the manipulating. Scoops then were used to lift and pack the butter in tubs or crocks.

Butter often was made from sour cream, but a sweet cream type also was produced. When a city buyer came to the farm, he would insert a long, thin tester in the butter. The tester bore down and extracted a narrow sample all the way to the bottom of the crock. The buyer examined this to be sure that the butter at the base was as good as that on top, with an even color and a non-oily texture.

Wooden butter molds and stamps with ornamental designs are considered treen objects. They are discussed in Chapter Nine.

Long ago, a housewife could not buy a cake of yeast at a store. Instead, she had to "catch" her own. Her trap might be a batter of flour, sugar, and salt stirred with water drained from cooked, peeled potatoes. This mixture was left uncovered for several hours. Tiny yeast plants float in the air, and some would enter the batter.

Yeasts are very simple fungus plants that multiply rapidly. Some grow through continuous budding. A small part of the cell wall swells until the protrusion breaks away from the parent plant to form a new cell. This in turn grows more buds. Some yeast plants increase by dividing in two. This method of securing cells was chancy because types of yeasts unsuitable for bread making might become lodged in the liquid.

It was possible to make yeast from hops, beer mash or its settlings boiled with potatoes. This was kept in an

Hops basket, metal bands, 31″ wide, 23″ deep, 19½″ high, circa 1850, **$120.** Iowa.

Dough tray (bowl), 19″ long, 12½″ wide, **$55.** Georgia.

earthenware jar, and some of the old was added to new batches of yeast so that its use was continuous down through the years. Neighbors occasionally borrowed yeast starter from each other if their supply ran out.

Bread was baked in batches sufficient to supply big families. Large dough bowls or boxes were required and were called trays or troughs. Loaves were put into the oven with the aid of a peel. The bread pan was placed on this flat surface, and by jiggling, was dislodged after it was inserted into the hot opening. It required deftness to scoop the pan onto the peel in order to remove it after the bread was baked.

Wooden slabs on which to cut loaves are ornamental with incised (cut in) strands of wheat or with the word "bread" standing out in bold relief. Many treen plates for this purpose are imported from England. They may be accompanied by a knife with a wooden handle which says "bread" on it. Constant hand pressure through the years has eradicated portions of the raised letters. Some moderns place these plates in wall groupings while others like to slice small loaves on them at the table as they dine.

Sugar is another edible that has changed through the years. Early in the 1800s, it came in cones, perhaps weighing fifty-five pounds apiece. Smaller ones with rounded tops that weighed about twelve pounds were called loaves. Housewives chipped off hunks with a hammer, and a special cutter or nipper created smaller pieces that could be placed in large covered bowls. Wooden examples are not easily obtainable today. Generally, granulated sugar, coarse and brown, was available after 1865. Because it hardened, a storekeeper needed an auger (a sharp, pointed tool with movable clenchers) to

64

Bread peel with initials "P. H. R." is 24″ long and 12½″ in diameter, **$125.** Iowa.

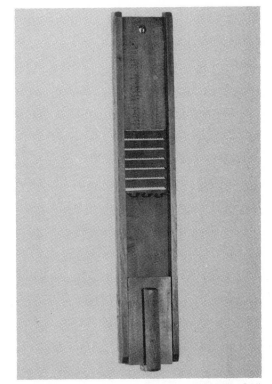

Vegetable slicer, patented Feb. 22, 1898, 21″ long, 3½″ wide, 1¾″ deep, **$45.** Illinois.

Breadboard and knife; board 10½″ diameter, 12″-long knife reads "Encore Thomas Turner & Co., Cutters to His Majesty," **$115** set. Illinois.

Rare sugar bowl for lump sugar, 10″ diameter, 9″ high, **$1,200.** Iowa.

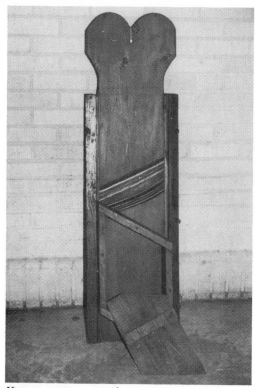

Kraut cutter, wooden pegs, Pennsylvania origin, communal use, 48″ long, 14″ wide, **$225.** Alabama.

Apple peeler, circa 1840, 10½″ long, 5½″ high, **$85.** Connecticut.

Apple peeler, early 1800s, 17½″ wide, 13¼″ deep, 4″ high; on the other side is a checkerboard which, when used, had to have a special surface to accommodate cutter parts of the apple peeler or it could have rested on the top of a barrel, **$138.** Connecticut.

Apple peeler, painted red, sits on table when used, 26″ long, **$250.** Iowa.

get it out of the shipping barrel and a grinder to pulverize it for his customers.

Food growing and preparation were constant chores in days of yore. Extra garden vegetables, berries, and fruits were preserved for winter use. Vegetable slicers frequently advertised in the late 1800s were listed in some catalogs as slaw or kraut cutters. Heads of cabbage were moved across the blades and came out through the bottom as shredded strips that were layered and salted well in huge, clean crocks with weights to hold down the cabbage. Its juice joined the salt to form a brine and fermented to make sauerkraut. This kept well for winter consumption.

Apples are a versatile fruit. They can be picked and eaten raw. They can be baked whole or sliced in pies, cookies, and cakes. They can be cooked to make apple butter, sauce, or jellies. In liquid form, they become apple juice, a spicy drink called cider, or vinegar for pickling and cooking.

Fresh whole apples kept well when stored in a cool, dry place where they could not freeze. This might be in a cellar under the house, or in a dry, earth-covered fruit cellar dug in a hillside. The apples were sorted occasionally, and those with soft or rotten spots were removed. In cold regions, batches of pies could be baked and placed in cupboards with punched tin panels that let ventilation in but kept rodents and flies out. The storage area could be an unheated attic where freezing would occur. Sides of meat also could be hung in the cold, and pieces would be sawed off as needed for winter consumption.

Apples were preserved by drying. The fruit was pared, quartered, cored, and then a large needle and stout thread were used to string them into lengths that could be hung up to dry. An alternative was to peel, slice the apples, and place them in one layer on a slatted frame or basket that was set in the sun so the fruit could dry. Soaking in a little water would plump the shriveled apples for winter use. The first apple peeler was patented in 1803. Later, metal ones were manufactured that cored and sliced them as well.

Neighbors could enjoy a social time together as they joined to prepare apple butter. Various people washed, peeled, cored, or sliced the fruit while others mixed and cooked. They used very long paddles to stir the apples, spices, sugar, and cider bubbling together in the huge kettles. It took five or six hours with plenty of stirring to cook down a batch, but the thick brown treat that resulted tasted good on freshly baked bread.

Wooden tableware was commonly

Treenware from left to right: large noggin, 9½" high, 4¼" diameter, **$200.** Smaller noggin, 7" high, 4¼" diameter, **$175.** Wooden bowl to the left, wafer thin, 6" diameter, **$225.** Trencher, 10½" diameter, **$250.** Iowa.

used, and plates — either round or square, big or little — were called trenchers. A man and his wife shared one, and the children did likewise. When a trencher has cuts and scrapes on both the top and the bottom, this indicates that it was flipped over at mealtime so that the top was used for the dinner side and the bottom served as the pie side. Stews, vegetables, and porridge were the usual foods that were dipped from the big kettles, so wooden bowls were available also. Noggins are wooden pitchers. Each one, handle and all, was carved out of a single block of wood. Everyone took a drink from the noggin as it was passed from person to person. Noggins also served as measuring cups. While spoons were available, fingers generally conveyed food to the mouth. Boxes abounded. It was helpful to be able to hang essential articles on the wall, out of the way, yet within easy reach. Coarse salt had to be placed in a mortar and pounded with a pestle to reduce it to useful grains. Often, it was kept in wall boxes. Spices, likewise, were hung up in containers. Spices came in seed and bulk form and might be pulverized before use, although some, such as nutmeg, were grated.

Round wooden spice boxes into which fit smaller boxes, each labeled for its contents, are less common than those made of tin.

A small room where kitchen supplies were kept was called a pantry, but many homes did not have this luxury. There were stacks of what are now termed pantry boxes. These were all-purpose

Salt box, 5½″ diameter, 9″ high, **$60.** Iowa.

Walnut salt box with heart and diamond applied decorations, 7¾″ wide, 5″ deep, 12″ high, **$145.** Illinois.

Hanging spice box with tilting bin, 13″ wide, 4″ deep, 10″ high, **$125.** Illinois.

containers because they varied greatly in sizes and often came in graduated nests. They could hold flour, butter, herbs, cheese, rye, cornmeal, soda, or spices. Pills might be stored in the smallest one or a man might place a pinch of snuff in a tiny type.

Knife boxes held cutlery, and there were scouring boxes in which ashes or pumice were put. The grit served to scour the knives.

A kitchen area usually had a comb case that hung on the wall near a washbasin so the family members could tidy up rapidly. Candle boxes, whether they hung or lay flat, held extra candles. Generally, they had lids because mice gnawed on tallow, and a cover deterred rodents. A smoker enjoyed having his pipe within easy reach, so a pipe box was hung near the fireplace. He could take his pipe out to puff on as he relaxed.

Grinders served throughout the 1800s. Since coffee was purchased in bean form, it had to be ground before it could be measured into a pot. Some people currently buy beans to grind daily for extra-fresh coffee. A more complicated grinder served for meats. It was handmade in North Carolina prior to the Civil War (1861–1865). Some farm family might have used it to make sausage.

Since many wooden objects were constructed at home by hand, they furnish much information about what was needed by people in the past. It is pleasant to find signs of wear that indicate some tool or bowl was a favorite, and it is fun to picture a family sharing trenchers or a noggin as they ate. Imagination, coupled with examples of treenware, helps link contemporary people with their American heritage.

Spice box, 8″ wide, 3″ deep, 12″ high, **$85.** Butter paddle, **$22.** Miniature jug on top of spice box reads ''Minnie Fairport, 1893,'' 3″ high, **$70.** Illinois.

Spice cabinet, lift-lid bottom bin, 11″ wide, 8″ deep bottom, 4¼″ deep top, 19″ high, **$225.** Illinois.

Spice cabinet, 12″ wide, 18″ high, **$115.** Iowa.

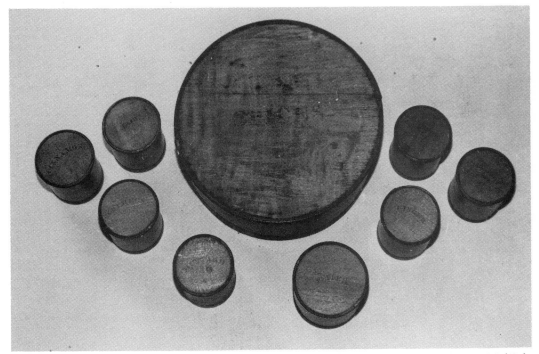

Round spice holder, 9¼″ diameter, 3¼″ high; small spice boxes, 2½″ diameter, 3″ high; larger individual box, 3½″ diameter, 3″ high, **$135.** Ohio.

Bucket bench, painted blue, origin Wisconsin, 28½" wide, 12½" deep at bottom, 47½" high, **$600.** Game board above bench (checkers on reverse side) 14" × 16", **$300.** Round pantry boxes, painted, **$85** to **$125.** Iowa.

Oval pantry boxes: bottom box 8½" wide, 7" deep, 3" high; top box 3½" wide, 2" deep, 1½" high; top, **$116.** Bottom, **$250.** Second from top, **$110.** Remaining four, **$145** each. Georgia.

Walnut knife box, dovetailed, 13" wide, 9½" deep, 6" high, **$55.** Illinois.

Grit box (scouring box) for sharpening knives with ashes or pumice, 9½″ wide, 4″ deep, 15½″ high, **$55.** Pennsylvania.

Use of this wall case was determined by owner, 9½″ wide, 4″ deep, 17″ high, **$95.** Illinois.

Scouring box (grit box) for sharpening knives with ashes or pumice, 10″ wide, 7″ deep, 3″ high, **$95.** Indiana.

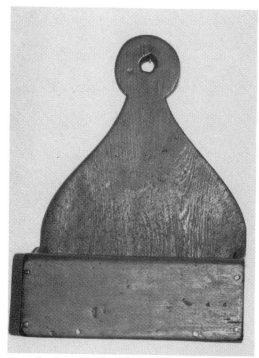

Candle box, painted green, keyhole top, 10¼″ wide, 6″ deep, 14½″ high, **$250.** Iowa.

Coffee grinder or mill, 6½″ square, 7½″ high, **$65.** Ohio.

Candle box, dated 1883, has original blue paint; sliding top used because mice chewed candles, 12″ wide, 8″ deep, 6″ high, **$125.** Georgia.

Box for pipes, brass knob on drawer, heart cutout, 5″ wide, 4½″ deep, 22″ high, **$650.** Iowa.

Folding bootjack, 20″ long collapsed, **$55.** Illinois.

Meat grinder, origin North Carolina, circa 1860, 12″ wide, 8″ deep, 8″ high, **$185.** Iowa.

Cobbler's shoe last, three pieces, two lasts, **$75.** Connecticut.

Treenware from left to right: sander signed "James Terring 1712" held white sand for blotting ink, 4″ diameter, 3½″ high, **$45.** Tidy top, a lamp stand for a betty lamp, **$110.** Burl mortar, 4½″ diameter, 4½″ high, **$85.** Iowa.

Walnut footstool, 14″ wide, 6″ deep, 7″ high, **$67.50.** Iowa.

Far wall: vegetable slicer, 10″ long, **$15.** Mitten dryer with thumb that pulls out, 16″ long, **$45.** Right wall: spice box, 10″ wide, 5″ deep, 7″ high, **$85.** Scrub box, 7″ wide, 11″ high, **$45.** Breadboard with handle, 16″ long, **$42.** Iowa.

Bed wrenches used to tighten ropes on rope beds: top 14½″×18″, **$45.** Bottom 16½″×13″ (replaced crosspiece) **$16.** Connecticut.

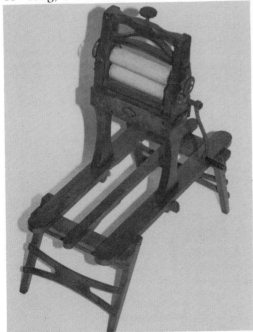

Prototype of wringer and wash bench (often called child's toy or salesman's sample) 12″ wide, 5½″ deep, 14″ high, **$175.** Tennessee.

Checkerboard, wooden frame supports two-piece board on which the alternate squares originally were painted black and the others left natural, 13″ wide, 19½″ deep, **$175.** Iowa.

Child's butter churn, 5½″ diameter top, 7½″ bottom, 11½″ high, **$75.** Connecticut.

Child's snow shovel, 34″ long, 7″ wide, 10½″ deep at base, **$75.** Illinois.

Dissected (difsected) map of England and Wales, early 1800s, grained box (individual parts of the jigsaw puzzles were made of wood upon which paper was applied) 11½″ wide, 9½″ deep, **$200.** Iowa.

Grain shovel, 36″ long, handle and bowl made in one piece, **$125.** Illinois.

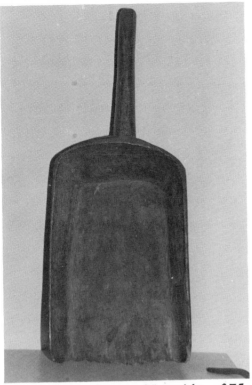

Scoop, 20″ long, 8″ wide, **$75.** Connecticut.

Farm shovel, 44″ long, 13½″ wide, 14″ deep, **$185.** Pennsylvania.

Clothing washtub also served as a child's bathtub, 25″ diameter, 17″ high, **$150.** Iowa.

Piggin (defined as a small wooden pail with one stave extended above the rim to serve as a handle) 12″ diameter, 13½″ high, **$235.** Ohio. *(Note:* A firkin is a small wooden tub for butter or lard, or a measure equal to one-quarter barrel.)

Peck and one-half peck measure: top peck cavity 10¼″ diameter; bottom one-half peck cavity 8¾″ diameter, 13½″ high, **$135.** Ohio.

Grain measure, one-half bushel, Hall & Taylor, Jamestown, N.Y., **$55.** Pennsylvania.

Grape picking basket has a flat back and when basket is full, it can be strapped to the back for carrying the load home, 19″ wide, 15″ deep, 27″ high, **$150.** Illinois.

Blueberry rake, 4½″ wide, 5¼″ deep, 19½″ high, **$175.** New York.

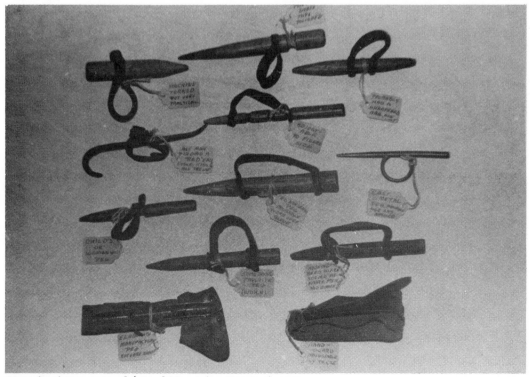

Corn husking pegs, **$4** to **$12** each. Pennsylvania.

Wooden stirrups: large, **$14.** Small, **$12.** Illinois.

Farrier carrier or blacksmith's tote tray, early 1800s, 22″ wide, 14″ deep, 8″ high, **$135.** Illinois.

4 Let your light shine

Lighting progressed very little from ancient times until the 1800s. There are no sharp cutoff dates when one type of lamp went out of style and a new kind was adopted. Instead, their use overlaps, and candles flickered continuously for thousands of years. This chart merely attempts to show general trends.

General Chart on Lighting

Approximate Date	Types of Lighting	Fuel
Colonial America 1607–1783 (Actually, many of these lighting devices continued in use well into the 1800s.)	Lamps: pan, crusies, double crusies, bettys	Vegetable and animal fat, fish oil*
	Rushlights	Rush dipped in grease
	Candles (continuously)	
1700s but peaked in 1830s . . . out about 1860	Whale oil lamps — often had one or two short metal tubes protruding for the wicks	Whale oil
Late 1700s	Lanterns — horn or glass sides in wooden or metal frames, originally called "lant horn" because panels were made of thin slices of horn boiled so light would pass through	Candle frequently, but some whale oil
1784 and well into 1800s	Argand lamp with cylindrical wick for better light	Oil, with early examples often using whale oil

*The American Indians taught colonists how to prepare fish oil for lamps. They also shared their knowledge of torches.

About 1784, the glass chimney was developed to protect flame from drafts. However, most lamps had open flame until about 1860.

The 1800s saw many patents issued for improvements in lamps and/or fuel.

1816	Baltimore, first American city to be lighted with manufactured gas	Manufactured gas
1820	Braided candlewick better than twisted	Candle
Early 1800s to about 1870	Peg lamp linked candles and lamps. Font had protrusion that fit into a candlestick socket; also called socket lamps	Whale oil, later kerosene
1824	Fredonia, N.Y., used natural gas from a nearby well	Natural gas
1830–1850	Burning fluid lamps, highly inflammable and explosive. Danger caused their demise. Differed from whale oil lamps because metal tubes for wicks were tall to keep flames away from fuel, and tubes slanted away from each other	Alcohol and turpentine mixed (camphine)
1840–1860	Lard lamp, not very successful, lard tended to solidify.	Melted lard, lard oil
1851	Spring-loaded candlestick — as the candle melted down, a spring pushed the candle top up so the flame could be seen	Candle
1859 through early 1900s	Kerosene lamps of all kinds developed after the first successful oil well was sunk into the ground	Kerosene
1875 into early 1900s	Student lamp with fuel reservoir higher than the burner	Kerosene
1879	Edison invented the incandescent bulb. The White House was electrified during President Benjamin Harrison's term (1889–1893)	Electricity

How exciting it must have been when man first learned how to build a fire. It protected him from cold, gave him light, allowed him to cook food, and, since some wild animals feared fire, it kept them from attacking. When man took a burning tree limb and held it aloft, he had a torch.

Some authorities have speculated on how the first lamp came to be. Only three things were needed — a container or font, a fuel, and a wick. Maybe a bit of animal grease fell in a hollow stone where a curled dry leaf lay. It could have been ignited accidentally from popping sparks from the fire. The stone was the font, the grease was the fuel, and the leaf was the wick. Eureka! A primitive lamp. After that, clay saucers baked hard in the sun could be lamps. Progress could continue until copper, brass, bronze, iron, tin, pewter, china, or glass was used.

Iron crusie grease lamp, mid-1600s, **$285.** Connecticut.

People in biblical times used candles, and their lamps were similar to those of colonial America. That's because for thousands of years, lighting changed very little. A pan lamp, a crude, early form of lighting, was a shallow, saucer-type vessel that held animal fat. A wick floating in it soaked up the grease and burned. Its light was feeble, smoky, and smelly. The fuel frequently seeped out, so the word messy applied as well. Often, there was a pointed prong attached that could be thrust into a wooden beam or in the log cabin's chinks to form a suspended light.

A crusie provided a groove for the wick to lie in, and a double crusie improved upon this because there were two pans, one above the other. This was a mess saver and a fuel saver because the lower layer caught the overflow drips, and could be returned to the upper pan for fuel. Some people term this latter a phoebe lamp, but many collectors do not feel this word applies. It's always a double crusie to them.

There is an unproven theory that the name betty lamp comes from a German word meaning better, which through the years has been slurred to become betty. This lamp shared bad qualities with the crusie, yet offered some advantages. The betty had a separate built-in tube in which the wick was held and elevated. This caused the fuel to run back into the font instead of seeping out. Betty lamps may or may not have hinged lids. Lids made them a little safer because the oil or grease was less apt to ignite when covered. Many bettys have wick picks attached that care for the wick by lifting it up if necessary, adjusting it, and eliminating charred portions. In the next photograph, an iron crusie is at the left. Next, the two pans of the iron double crusie (phoebe) are sitting one inside the other. And the wick channel on the tin betty is easy to see. It looks as if it is sticking out its tongue. This lamp is unusual because iron bettys are more common than tin ones.

Rush lights will be discussed later because they are distantly akin to candles, but a holder is pictured for this kind of light. Hanging versions are rare. The next lamp is a brass pan variety on a trammel while the third is a pan lamp of iron. The brass betty hanging from the iron trammel includes a wick pick.

A lamp with a betty-type top is unusual in pewter. A drip pan is midway down. A lamp similar to this was available in the 1700s, but this one is dated 1865, indicating that styles persisted for an extensive period of time.

A major development in lighting took place in 1784 when a Swiss scientist, Aimé Argand, took out a patent in England on a lamp that had a burner with a cylindrical wick that allowed air to reach the wick from both inside and out, thus producing more light. An assistant of Argand's found that a glass chimney protected the flame from drafts, but most lamps retained their open flames until about 1860. Many whale oil lamps adopted the Argand burner.

Whale oil was expensive in the late 1700s because much of it was imported from other countries. In the 1800s, American ships began to join the hunt for whales, and the United States became the leading whaling nation from about 1830 through the 1880s. The popularity of this fuel for lamps peaked in the 1830s and declined after kerosene became available in about 1859. Some lamps that used whale oil were made of a combination of blown glass and blown three-mold glass. For example, note the

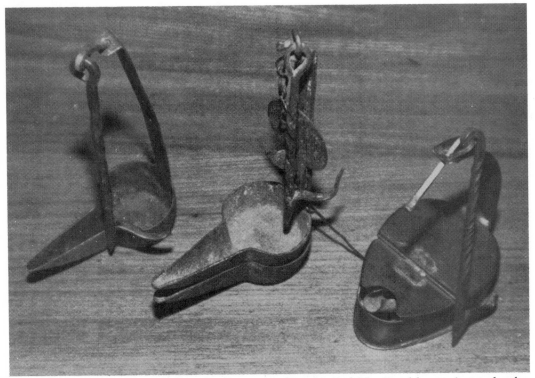

Metal lamps, left to right: crusie, bowl 2″ × 4″, 6½″ high, **$85.** Double crusie or phoebe, bowl 2″ × 4½″, 6½″ high, **$100.** Tin betty (notice wick channel that distinguishes it from a crusie), bowl 2½″ × 3¾″, **$125.** Each lamp has a hook used to fasten or hang the lamp over an object. Iowa.

Betty lamp with wick channel, bowl 2½" × 3½", **$115.** Illinois.

Pewter betty lamp with drip pan midway on shaft, dated 1865, 8½" high, **$235.** Illinois.

Lighting devices, left to right: hanging rush light, iron, 21" long, **$295.** Brass pan lamp, on iron trammel, 29½" long, **$345.** Pan lamp, iron, 23" long, **$175.** Betty lamp, brass, on iron trammel, 24¼" long, **$350.** Iowa.

Top of betty lamp showing date, 1865, and wick channel.

Glass whale oil lamps, left: central wick tube, base diameter 3½″, height 6½″, **$100.** Right: blown font and molded base, double wick tube, circa 1820, 2½″ square base, 8½″ high, **$250.** Iowa.

Whale oil lamp, green glass, threaded burner collar of pewter, single wick tube, circa 1820, 8½″ high, 3¾″ base width, **$200.** Iowa.

tall lamp at the right with a font that was blown by human lung power. Its base was blown into a mold. The two were heated at the point of contact, and since glass melts, they became fused. During the 1840s, attractive lamps were made from blown fonts and lacy pressed bases. Collars, circle outlines of pewter that screwed over threaded burners, were known in Europe earlier, but came into being in America in about the 1820s. A plaster material attached them securely.

Some whale oil lamps were made of painted tin (tole), which emulated Oriental lacquer work and was referred to as japanned. A petticoat lamp flared out at the base, almost as if it were really a gathered undergarment for the wide skirts of a woman of the 1800s. It could stand upright or had a round tube underneath that could fit into the socket of a candlestick to give the stubby lamp height. This tube also could be slipped over the side upright of a chair as a man sat to read or a women sewed. There were lamps with a side slot so that a pin could be inserted to push the wick up as needed in order to facilitate burning.

The burning fluid lamp was greeted with praise when it came out in 1830. Its light was bright, clean, and odorless but, unfortunately, it had a Dr. Jekyll-Mr. Hyde personality. Whale oil did not demand special care. Burning fluid, a combination of alcohol and turpentine, was tempermental, highly inflammable, explosive, and deadly. There were so many accidents involving serious burns and fatalities that there were those who felt the government should outlaw it. By 1850, it lost its sales appeal. Consumers didn't want it.

There are various ways to distinguish a burning fluid lamp from the whale oil variety. The round tubes that hold the wicks upright differ. Whale oil ones stand straight and short on top and descend down into the fluid. Not so the explosive variety. Measures were taken to keep the heat and flame away from the volatile oil. The tubes sit high, away from the fuel. They slant away from each other so that the heat is not concentrated. In addition, since alcohol evaporates readily, there are frequently lids attached by chains that cap the tubes when the lamp is not lighted. They can also serve as extinguishers since it is dangerous to blow the flame. Turpentine and camphine are synonymous, so people tend to call these lamps camphine, but this is an error. A few camphine lamps (turpentine alone) were made, but the correct term for the turpentine-alcohol mixture is burning fluid, according to the patent issued.

The name *spark* is a descriptive title applied to a type of small whale oil lamps. Spark, a noun, is an old-fashioned term for a gallant man, a beau or lover. To spark, a verb, means to woo or court. This was not substantiated by

Burning fluid lamp, four angled wick tubes with covers to prevent evaporation of alcohol and to extinguish flames, circa 1830, 4½" diameter, 8" high, **$175.** Iowa.

Whale oil lamps: left background, brass with adjustment slot in tin wick tube, 2½" diameter, 5½" high, **$135.** Right background, petticoat lamp, tole, could be fastened in candlestick socket or over the ear of a chair by using tube in base of lamp, 2½" diameter, 4¾" high, **$175.** Foreground, finger grip lamp with tole painting, 2½" diameter, 2¼" high, **$75.** Iowa.

Green glass sparking lamp, whale oil, 2″ diameter, 4″ high, **$200.** Iowa.

Brass lucerna lamp, used olive oil, two spouts, with wick pick, extinguisher, and tweezers, 4½″ diameter, 19″ high (raises and lowers in height), **$250.** Iowa.

Clear glass sparking lamp with wick tube cover and extinguisher, circa 1850, 4½″ high, **$185.** Illinois.

Tin lard lamp, flat wick in tall cylinder, patented by J. Stonesifer, Aug. 8, 1854, 6½″ diameter, 8″ high, **$85.** Georgia.

any of the books consulted that discussed lighting, but a romantic folk-type tale persists that a sparking lamp was lighted when a young gentleman came to call on his chosen lady friend. Since the font was small, the lamp would not burn for an extended period of time. When its light began to dim, the youth had been there long enough. It was time for him to go home.

Olive oil fills the font of a lucerna, a brass lamp from Italy. Most have three or four burners, but two spouts are considered unusual. Dangling from chains are necessary articles that keep the flame flickering brightly. A wick pick pries at the wick, the tweezers pull it up, the snuffer trims it, and the extinguisher puts out the light. The lucerna has its own intensive care unit included with the price of purchase.

Melted lard or lard oil served as an inexpensive fuel from about 1840–1860, but it was not too satisfactory because it tended to solidify and refuse to burn. Methods were devised to keep it up near the flame so it would remain in a liquid state. A lamp patented by J. Sonesifer is

dated August 8, 1854. The lard was poured in the circular reservoir and was forced up in the spout wick area by a screw-driven piston. This was one of the many patents issued for lamp and fuel improvements in the 1800s as advances in lighting were sought.

Pewter spout lamp, 12″ high, **$210.** Illinois.

Pewter is not a mined metal. Instead, it is an alloy created by combining tin with copper, lead, antimony, and occasionally bismuth.

When there is a high tin content, pewter shines more brightly and, unless it is too tinny, is a better quality product. Lead is duller. This alloy is soft and dents or melts easily. The pewter spout lamp shown has a man-shaped finial. Some sources refer to a similar lamp as a rabbi's lamp or pastor's lamp. No reason is given for the names.

Peg lamps, left to right: clear font, **$175.** Blue flowers on font, inserted in candlestick, **$175.** Frosted font, **$175.** Each 6¼″ high. Iowa.

Peg lamps are transitional pieces. They link candles and lamps together. Because a prong (a peg or a stump) extending down in the center of the font could be

Rush light, molded ratchet can be adjusted in height from 45½" to 57", wood and iron, no price available. Iowa.

Rush light, wooden base 4½" diameter, 15½" high; this later rush light has a holder for a candle, **$175.** Iowa.

placed in the socket of a fine, sturdy candlestick to form an attractive lamp, the idea appealed to frugal housewives. They could use favorite candleholders for their bases, have attractive lamps, and save money. In England these lamps are known as socket lamps. Many burned whale oil.

Another next-of-kin to candles are rush lights. They were made from marsh plants that were picked when they were mature but still green. They were allowed to dry. With the exception of a layer to hold the pith together, the leaves and skin were stripped to expose the core. These were dipped or soaked in grease, tallow, mutton fat, or in the fat of wild animals, and hung up to harden. When in use, a rushlight was suspended at a forty-five-degree angle in a metal holder that clenched it midway. The top, or in some cases, both ends, were lighted. Rushlights helped illuminate colonial homes and were used into the 1800s. Best of all, they cost almost nothing. When pinched in a floor model ratchet, the height could be adjusted readily. If a candleholder was included with the rush attachment, it proved convenient, and represented a later model stand. Don't buy a converted Mexican branding iron as a rush holder. Does the socket for the candle resemble those on a candlestick? It should.

Basically, there are two ways to make candles. They can be formed by repeated dippings in melted tallow, or the tallow can be poured into molds to harden. Dipping is the older method.

In the late fall, when beef cattle were butchered for the family's winter supply of meat and for their hides, all scrap fat was saved to melt down into tallow. On candle-making day, these scraps were placed in a kettle of boiling water, and when the tallow rose to the top, it was skimmed off. The process was repeated to clear the tallow of impurities. It was kept in a melted state. If candles slightly less than nine inches long were to be made, the wicking was wound repeatedly on a board nine inches long, and when it was full, one end was cut through so that eighteen-inch pieces remained. These were doubled over the candle rods and the two strands of each were twisted into one cord, now about nine inches in length. Perhaps there would be six wicks on eight rods for a total of forty-eight. Two chairs of the same height were placed a slight distance apart, and two supporting poles were put across their top rails. These served as the frame across which the smaller rods (with their wicks hanging down) were placed.

One at a time, six-strand rods were dipped into the tallow in the kettle. When a rod had a first coat clinging to it, it was hung over the poles to harden, and the next rod was dipped. By the time all eight had been submerged, the first one would be ready for its second coating. The process continued until the candles were of the thickness desired. A pan on the floor caught any drips, which were returned to the kettle. An even temperature had to be maintained. If the kettle was too hot, the tallow would melt from the wicks instead of building up. If it was too cold, it would not cling well. The candles would be hung to harden thoroughly before they were placed in a candle box and packed away in a cool spot. Beeswax taken from hives or bayberries picked from bushes could be used in place of beef fat.

A special stand sometimes speeded up the dipping process. It had revolving arms on which wicks were placed at intervals. The whole arm was removed from the stand and dipped at one time, replaced, and the next arm was submerged until all wicks received the required number of coats.

Candle dipper with two crosspieces that lift off, turned pedestal base with three legs, late seventeenth century or early eighteenth century, 22″ wide, 23″ high, **$800.** Iowa.

Candle dipper, 9″ diameter base, 28″ high, **$72.** Iowa.

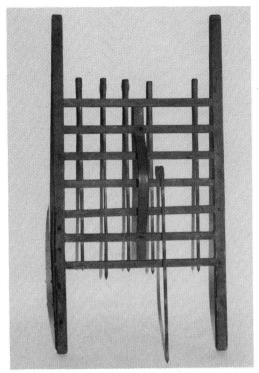

Candle dryer, with handle and removable drying rods (notice that one has been removed), 11″ × 20½″, **$295.** Iowa.

Brass pricket candlestick, 7″ high. This type speared the base of the candle to hold it erect and predates the socket type. **$100.** Iowa.

Rods, wicking, and a mold in a supporting frame were needed for molding. For a twelve-tube mold, six pieces of wicking would be looped over each of two rods in the same manner as they were for dipping. A rod would be held so that the wicking would drop into six tubes and go out the tiny holes at the tapered ends. Some people held the wicks taut and straight by placing a piece of potato over the points. The other six tubes would be threaded in the same way, and the hot tallow would be poured into the mold that would be set out-of-doors to cool. When the candles hardened, the mold would be brought in and dipped quickly in hot water to loosen them. The rods with six candles attached would be lifted out of the mold. The wicks then were trimmed and the process was repeated until enough candles were prepared to supply the family's needs.

Holders for candles may be made of pottery, china, glass, wood, or metals. They may be plain and utilitarian or ornate and decorative. An early form had a pricket, which speared the center of the base of a candle to hold it erect. It predated the socket style in which a candle fits into a small cup. Various features sometimes increased a candle-holder's usefulness. For example, some were made with ejectors so that the candle could be pushed up as it became smaller. Thus, even the last little nub could be burned, and any small bit retained in the holder could be flipped out and melted again when a new supply of candles was made.

The projection that permitted the candlestick to be hung over the back of the chair or on a loom to give a worker light was referred to as a spur. This practice helps explain why chair backs are found with the outline of a flame burned into the wood.

When a reflector was placed in back

Twelve-tube candle mold, 15″ handle to
handle, 10″ high, **$55.** Connecticut.

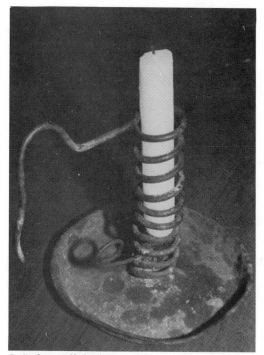

Spiral candleholder with metal saucer has
an ejector that twists up through the coils,
raising the candle's height, and a spur that
can be attached to the back of a chair, circa
1750, 5″ diameter, 4¾″ high, **$75.** Iowa.

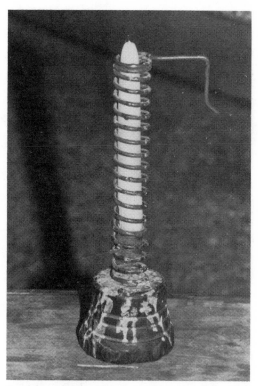

Spiral candleholder with wooden base has
a twisting ejector and spur, 11″ high, **$125.**
Illinois.

95

of a candle, it helped to increase the amount of light. A spring-loaded candleholder known as a student, reading, or lacemaker's lamp had a hooded reflector that concentrated the light much as a spotlight does. The candle was inserted at the bottom and was supported by a spring and a plate so that, as the wax burned down, the candle would be pushed up. This spring-loaded candleholder was publicly displayed at London's Great Exhibition in 1851 when many such exciting newcomers were featured in the huge glass Crystal Palace hall. Queen Victoria's beloved husband, Prince Albert, donated much time and energy to this world attracting event. It influenced home decorating styles for many years.

Birdcage candlestick, wooden base, sliding candle socket with friction grip that can adjust the candle's height, eighteenth century, 8½″ high, **$145.** Iowa.

Brass beehive candlesticks: front, left and right, 6¾″ high, **$175.** Pair. Larger pair in rear, 9″ high, **$225.** Front center, 9″, **$125.** Iowa.

Brass lacemaker's lamp, spring-loaded to raise the candle's height, hooded reflector concentrates the light on a specific area, circa 1850, 15″ high. An English writer calls this a student or reading candlestick. **$185.** Iowa.

Ratchet, floor model candleholder with wooden base, tin candleholders, adjusts from 24″ to 37″ high, **$1,000.** Iowa.

Left: tin chamber stick to light the way to the bedchamber at night, 5″ high, **$45.** Right: iron ejector hog scraper candlestick, 7″ high, **$75.** Connecticut.

Wrought iron candleholder, 11½″ wide, 21½″ high, **$200.** Connecticut.

Wedding band, hog scraper candlesticks with ejector lever (called wedding band because of the brass rings), **$400** each. Ohio.

Black japanned tin chamber stick, patented Dec. 3, 1912, 5¼″ diameter, 1¼″ high, **$25.** Ohio.

Another handy item was the chamber stick. Its purpose was to light the way to the bedchamber at night. At first, it was a saucerlike arrangement, but later a finger loop was added at the base to make it easier to carry. Also useful was a hog scraper candlestick with a double-duty function. After swine were butchered in the fall, their carcasses were dipped in boiling water and the bristles had to be scraped off. The underside of the candleholder could be used for this purpose. After that, it could be taken inside the house and set on the table. With a candle in it, it provided light for the family. A push-up ejector in a slot kept the candle available as it burned down to a stub.

Lanterns were carried out-of-doors. Pierced tin lanterns protected the flame of a candle from drafts and were used from about 1820–1850. The light they shed was not robust. For this reason, they could not be used efficiently, but their patterns were attractive. The little holes and slits in the tin allowed air to enter so the candle could burn. However, not much light passed through the perforations. Some people mistakenly believe this is a Paul Revere lantern. This is not based on fact. The historic ride to warn the colonists that the British were coming took place in 1775, and this noted patriot died in 1818. The lantern was not available in 1775, nor even in 1818 since it was introduced about 1820. In addition, a glass lantern from which rays would radiate to be seen readily would be needed to send a signal from the steeple of Boston's Old North Church to a waiting watcher far below. Because a punched tin lantern is stingy when it comes to shedding its light afar, it would have been very difficult to see.

A retired farmer states that small lanterns that swing on a handle frequently are misnamed. While many think they lighted the way for skaters on ice-

Brass ejector chamber stick, 6″ × 7″ base, 4″ high, **$75.** Ohio.

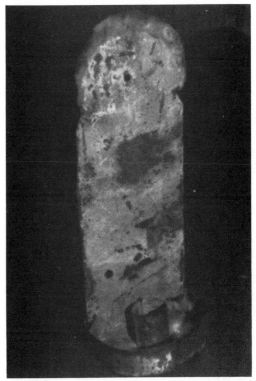

Tin wall sconce (sconces were in back of candles to reflect a brighter light), 3½″ wide, 10″ high, **$95.** Iowa.

Tin ejector chamber stick with red and yellow stenciled design, 4¾″ diameter, 3½″ high, **$27.50.** Ohio.

Double tin wall sconce, 7½″ wide, 13″ high, **$130.** Iowa.

covered ponds or streams after dark, the farmer and his wife say they were privy lanterns. The wife claims that people in town were modest and didn't want neighbors to know when they went to the outhouse at night, so they carried only a small light. The man snorted, "Huh, I carried a big lantern and set it between my feet to keep them warm." His wife reminded him that he was raised on a farm without any neighbors nearby, so he didn't have to seek privacy at the privy. To this couple, the skater's lantern is a dainty version with a chain attached that could be interlaced through the fingers. This does seem logical. As a girl glided over the ice, she would have more control over a chain-held, petite lantern than one on an extended swaying handle.

Another specialized lantern folded, and a dealer facetiously dubs it a flashlight because it's so easy to carry. It can be folded and tucked away in a coat pocket when not needed. It is an example of toleware (tin), with the paint still intact. The panels are of mica (minerals that crystallize in thin layers that let light through). The term isinglass is some times heard also. The lantern was patented by a man named Minor on January 24, 1865. A later, larger version bears a 1908 date.

Lanterns with large lenses that concentrated the beam have been called bull's-eye. A small one, seen on page 102, might have lighted the path of the town night watchman as he patrolled the streets calling out, "All's well!"

A gimbal lantern had fun. It went to political parades when men (women didn't vote then) marched and noisily shouted out songs about the virtues of the candidate they supported. It sailed the seven seas visiting exotic ports. Its base was weighted so that it always swung into an erect, upright position. This helped. If a man stumbled, his lamp did not spill oil or grease on those around him. Some tin ones were painted with patriotic symbols or bore the name of the candidate. When an election wasn't in the offing, these lamps could go on fishing trips because it was easy to force the wooden handle down in the earth along the river bank.

Tin trivet-base swinging candleholder, early 1900s, 8½″ long, **$30.** Iowa.

Punched tin candle lantern, 15½" high, $85. Connecticut.

Kerosene lanterns, nineteenth century, called skater's or privy lanterns or other names according to use, 11¾" high, $65 each. Ohio.

Left: rare wooden crusie, 10½" high, circa 1865, unpriced. Right: folding tin lantern with space for extra candles and matches, asphaltum tole, $95. Iowa.

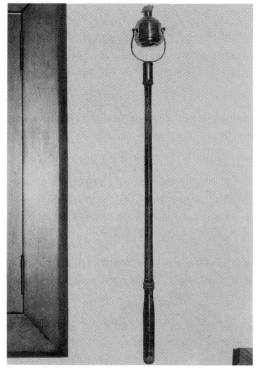

Folding tin candle lantern, patented 1908, 4½″ wide, 10″ high, **$145.** Iowa.

Gimbal (parade) lantern, brass font, 29″ long, **$45.** Illinois.

Bull's-eye lanterns: left, whale oil burner removed from lantern, 3″ diameter, 7″ high, **$140.** Right: kerosene burner removed from signal lantern, 3¾″ diameter, 8″ high, **$60.** Iowa.

When a miner was down underground working, he needed light, and he had to keep his hands free in order to sling a pick or manage a shovel. Because of this, a miner's lamp often had a sharp pricket attached that could be thrust into the side of the shaft somewhere. Other versions fastened on a hat or had other provisions for suspension. "Sticking tommy" was a name applied to a candleholder with a prong that miners plunged into beams.

Today, anything associated with railroad lore is a nostalgic collectible because chugging locomotives and the cars they pulled are no longer as prevalent as they once were. Some spout lamps are known as work lanterns. Can't you picture a brakeman kneeling by a wheel to try to locate a hotbox (an overheated bearing on the axle)? His search after dark could be helped if he carried a spout lamp.

When a bit of memorabilia bears the name of a particular railroad line, it is even more eagerly greeted as worthy of preserving. A railroad lantern, with 1907 as its latest patent date, fits in this category. It's from the Rock Island Lines.

An elderly lady recalls her childhood when her widowed mother sent the children out to taunt the railroad men as a train passed through town. Their object was to annoy the train's fireman, whose job it was to shovel coal into the furnace in order to keep up the steam level in the engine. Supposedly, he would become angry and toss coal at them, and they would carry the lumps home. Maybe he realized they needed to be warm and threw out coal for them to gather. If the fireman was, indeed, unfriendly, the crew members who ate and slept in the caboose weren't. Children waved at them as the train clattered by, and the railroaders' hands were always raised to acknowledge the greet-

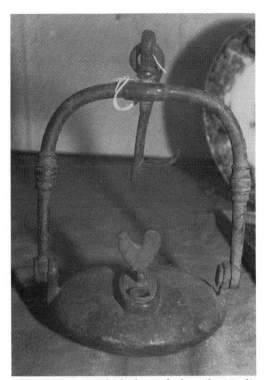

Cast iron miner's light, whale oil, 5″ diameter, 7″ high, **$160.** Colorado.

Brass and iron coal miner's lantern, circa 1915, Scranton, Penn., 2¾″ diameter, 9″ high, **$125.** Iowa.

Work lanterns or early railroad lamps, left to right: spout lamp, 4½″ diameter, 11½″ high, **$75.** Spout lamp, 1½″ diameter, 3″ high, **$45.** Spout lamp, 4″ diameter, 8½″ high, **$75.** Iowa.

Rock Island Lines railroad lantern made by the Adams & Westlake Co., patented 1907, 8″ wide, 9½″ deep, 14″ high, **$95.** Iowa.

ing. The end car on the train needed lights. One type was attached to the wall, and had a spring to force up the candle as it burned and was consumed. This kept the flame always in sight. Another is an oil lamp of tin that has a tin reflector in back of it. Reflectors served a double purpose. They not only increased the light sent out, but also protected the wall from the heat of the flame.

Horse-drawn vehicles and automobiles that were driven after dark required lights. Frequently, fixtures had a provision so that they could be clamped on. When the destination was reached, the lantern could be removed and used to light the way to the house or to the barn where the horse was cared for. The fancier brass lanterns were used on carriages.

Railroad car lanterns with spring-loaded candleholders, 15″ high, **$125** each. Iowa.

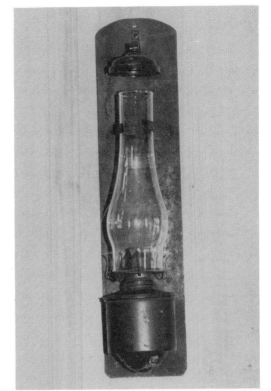

Railroad car lantern (may have been used in the caboose), has tin font and tin backing, was made by Dressel R. R. Lamp & Signal Co., Arlington, New Jersey, 5″ wide, 21″ high, **$95.** Ohio.

The horseless carriages, as the early automobiles were named, could have brass lamps, too. An early Maxwell side lamp, model 22, was made by the Knickerbocker Brass Goods Co. of New York.

A kerosene car lamp dated December 9, 1908, was manufactured of brass by E & J in the automobile city of Detroit, Michigan. In the back is a red reflector. The lamp shed its light to the side and front, and clear reflectors helped it cast a better glow in those directions.

A very specialized lantern was constructed to be closed up so that it would not emit light. Photographers who have to develop negatives in darkrooms found such a lantern necessary. It re-

Railroad car lantern, 15″ high, **$90.** Iowa.

Kerosene buggy lantern, has corrugated reflector, 6″ wide, 5″ deep, 13½″ high, **$85.** Iowa.

minds one of the Bible lamps that could be closed so that only a small path of light escaped at the bottom. Supposedly, during periods in history when believers were forbidden to read the Bible, some individuals were brave enough to defy the law. They had these lights with their almost invisible beam to aid them in their secretive study of the Bible.

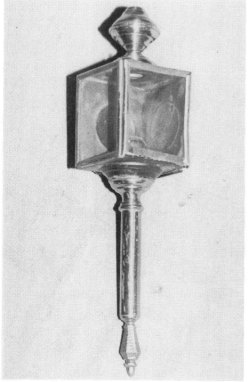

Brass and iron carriage lantern, 13″ high, **$75.** Iowa.

Brass Maxwell side lamp, model 22, made by Knickerbocker Brass Goods Co., New York, 11½″ high, **$150.** Illinois.

Kerosene automobile lamp, brass, made by E. & J., Detroit, Mich., Dec. 9, 1908, 13″ high, **$150.** Iowa.

Tin candle lantern with mica panels, circa 1830, 4½″ square, 12½″ high, **$95.** Iowa.

Darkroom lantern, 2½″ wide, 1½″ deep, 6″ high, **$52.** Connecticut.

Tin candle lantern for outdoor use, glass panels on three sides, lift lid, 14½″ square, 32½″ high, **$145.** Ohio.

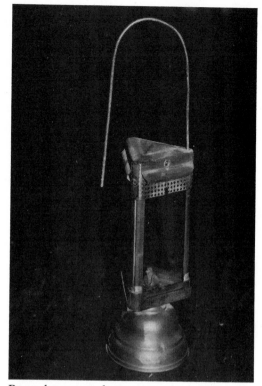

Tin candle lantern, three glass sides with one that slides up for access to light or to remove candle, dated 1853, 16″ high, **$165.** Connecticut.

Brass kerosene lantern made by Holmes, Booth & Haydens, Waterbury, Connecticut. 14½″ high, **$140.** Connecticut.

Carbide lamps (water was added to solid fuel). Left: brass, 2¼″ diameter, 4″ high, **$35.** Right: tin, 4″ wide, 3½″ deep, 8½″ high, **$60.** Iowa.

Brass student lamp, 20½″ high, **$375.** Illinois.

After the first petroleum well was drilled successfully in 1859, kerosene, one of its by-products, became a popular fuel for lamps. Its eager acceptance helped cause the decline of the whaling industry because it was less expensive and gave a better light than whale oil. Kerosene had no offensive odor or smoke. A student lamp that burns kerosene is related to the whale oil astral lamp that was developed about 1800. In an astral lamp, a horizontal arm extended from the shaft and supported the burner so that it was lower than the fuel reservoir. It was designed partly to decrease the size of the shadows cast by other lamps. Like the astral, the student lamp has a projecting arm, and the burner is lower than the container for the kerosene. It was in vogue from about 1875 to the early 1900s. Authorities feel brass examples are older than those with a nickel plating over brass.

When a silver solution was put in the

Pierced tin lantern, japanned finish, three glass and one pierced tin side, 6″ square, 16″ high, **$200.** Iowa.

Kerosene angle lamp, copper and brass, circa 1840, 13″ deep, 13″ high, **$250.** Ohio.

Reflector lamp with cast iron holder, mercury reflector, 18″ high, **$95.** Illinois.

space between two layers of blown clear glass, silvered or mercury glass resulted. This glass reacts to heat and cold readily and should be protected from rapid changes in temperature. It should be wrapped when it is taken out in the cold or, in summer, should be shielded from the hot rays of the sun. If the seal is broken, the glass loses its sheen and is no longer attractive. Because mercury glass is shiny, it reflects well. Hanging metal swinging brackets with such reflectors attached held kerosene lamps frequently.

When Thomas A. Edison invented the incandescent bulb in 1879, lighting entered a new era. The White House was electrified during President Benjamin Harrison's term in office (1889–1893). He was afraid to turn the switches on or off, so an attendant performed this service. Soon, whole cities were lighted by electricity. After thousands of years of little progress, lamps suddenly no longer resembled those in existence during Biblical times.

Collectors who enjoy lighting from past eras warn that value can be destroyed when people electrify old lamps through drilling or changing them. They suggest running wires up the outside to keep the old intact. This retains the antique flavor and the true link with history.

5 Stoneware

Stoneware sounds tough. It is referred to as hard paste based on its ability to scratch iron. It rings like quality flint glass when tapped, and is non-porous. Water does not get through its vitreous (glasslike) surface even when it is not glazed. Conversely, the poorer quality soft-paste wares can be scratched by iron and must be glazed in order to hold water. A red clay flowerpot is an example of a soft-paste article.

Stoneware is a form of folk art. Until the late 1800s, it was handmade on a potter's wheel. Some early examples were incised (design cut in) or stamped, but generally, untrained artists applied the decorations; their first choice was floral motifs.

A stroke here, a dot there, or a few swirls or squiggles represented flowers. Quick marks depicted birds, animals, patriotic emblems including eagles, occasional scenes, and people. Cobalt blue held up well under the high-heat firing (up to 2300 degrees Fahrenheit) necessary to make this hardware. The results from other colors were not always to be trusted, partly because they changed when fired; thus, the faithful true blue hue was utilized.

Perhaps you can place your thumb in the print left where a worker exerted pressure to apply a handle to the soft, wet, unbaked body of a newly formed crock or jug, or feel the ridges of glaze formed by slip trailed by a slip cup. An artist's rapid brushstroke may have been feathered out by a blue-smeared finger and the effort still shows. These are homemade touches. This combination of potter and painter meant each piece was an original. There could be a whole row of jugs or crocks with a symbolic flower pattern brushed on, but no two would be precisely alike because each was created and decorated individually.

Stoneware was made to serve a purpose. Each autumn, after the beef and hogs were butchered for the winter's meat supply, the farmer's wife stored salt

Scarce Bennington Factory ovoid crock, 1823, **$700.** Vermont.

pork and beef, plus her homemade mincemeat and lard in large crocks. The sauerkraut, pickled vegetables, and her own churned butter were already in their stoneware vessels. Apple juice, cider, and vinegar went into jugs. Town wives also stored food in stoneware for winter use. Storekeepers sold in bulk, and a customer could carry home a stoneware jug or bottle of molasses and keep the container. Its smooth surface was easy to wash and to keep clean.

111

Ovoid jar with lid, L. Norton, Bennington, 1828–1833, **$475.** Vermont.

L. Norton & Son jug, 1833–1840, **$275.** Vermont.

Stoneware is safe. Acids do not bother it, and it does not contaminate its contents. The salt glaze is pure and nontoxic. Earthenware, made of common clay by a simple process, was fashioned into useful pieces. Since it is porous, it is waterproofed by adding a glaze. One with a lead content was commonly used, a poison recognized as dangerous even prior to 1800. Food should not be stored in wares with a lead glaze, and they never should be used for eating purposes.

Stoneware has been around for hundreds of years. Some came from Europe with the earliest colonists who began to produce their own in the early 1700s. As that century closed, there were many potters who made stoneware.

Soft-paste pottery could be made of clay dug up in almost any locale. Not so the hard paste. It required the best clay, and that is kaolin (decomposed feldspar). It usually is white. On the East Coast, a top quality type came from Amboy, New Jersey. A clay that is slightly less sought after and less expensive was available from Long Island, New York. The Hudson River served a dual purpose. It provided transportation via boats for the raw material to be shipped to points along the banks and for the finished products to reach their markets. Because of this, potteries existed in New York State, New England, as well as in New Jersey. After the Erie Canal of some three hundred and fifty miles opened in 1825, the two New York cities of Albany on the Hudson River and Buffalo on Lake Erie were connected by a water route. The boats plied the Great Lakes, and opened the Midwest to easy access. Potteries established in that area were able to receive shipments of fine New Jersey clay. Previously, the price paid for overland hauling by horse and wagon had become too costly and too limited

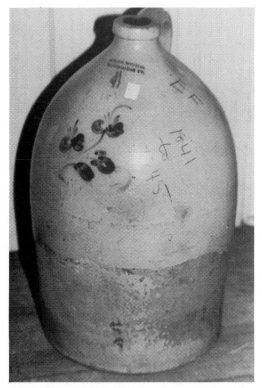

Jug, Julius Norton, Bennington, Vt., 1841–1845, **$195.** Vermont.

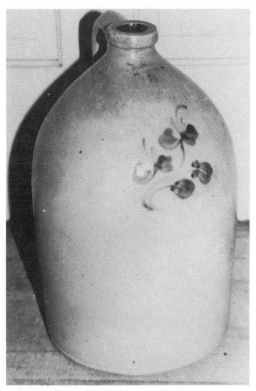

Jug, Julius Norton, Bennington, Vt., 1841–1845, **$300.** Vermont.

in the amount carried to permit quality clay to reach the interior.

The clay was dry and hard packed by the time it reached its destination. A machine broke it up and mixed it with water and sand (fine white silica) to add bulk, and with a binder to help prevent the pottery products from cracking and breaking. Next, it was necessary to strain out the stones and the hard lumps that refused to be pulverized.

When the clay was able to be molded or shaped, it was turned over to the master potter, or the thrower as he was called. He was so skilled at his job that he could complete a vessel in less than five minutes, and he could produce several hundred pieces per day. He had to be well coordinated.

His feet provided the power to turn

Jar, lid missing, Julius Norton, Bennington, Vt., 1841–1845, **$195.** Vermont.

Crock by E. & L. P. Norton, Bennington, 1861–1881. The customer's name, Anthony & Burlingame, Adams, Mass., a grocer, was impressed in the wet clay, **$250.** Vermont.

Crock, Julius Norton, Bennington, Vt., 1841–1845; brown Albany slip was used to glaze the inside of this crock, **$300.** Vermont.

the wheel upon which he threw and centered his bulk of clay, and his hands were working rapidly at the same time. He kept them wet as he hollowed out the lump. Next, with the aid of wooden tools, he shaped and raised the sides of the piece from the base up until it was time to form the rim of a crock or the narrow neck of a jug. Next, the surface was smoothed carefully with a damp cloth.

There are excellent cooks who, through experience, have a knack for adding a pinch of this or a handful of that to create tasty food. The thrower resembles such a cook. He knows how large his glob of clay must be. He may have a height and diameter gauge or calipers to help him size his vessel, but he judges mainly with his eyes and the feel of the clay. His jar can be neither too thin nor too thick. Like a cook's gravy, his resulting pottery must be smooth, exactly right, proportioned precisely.

Bakers have pastry tubes that press out strings of dough through an opening. A similar device served the potter as he forced out clay to be cut to the desired size to form a handle. He applied this to the body of the stoneware by pressing it into place with his thumbs, and his prints remained visible on the finished product. Following a final damp-cloth smoothing, the wet clay was hand stamped with the name of the company and/or that of a leading customer, if the article was for a special firm.

In a large pottery there might be a division of duties so that a finisher would smooth the vessel and another would apply the handles. This freed the thrower to begin the process all over again on another wheel.

When the newly formed article was semi-dry, it was soft enough to have designs incised (cut into) the surface at precisely even depths. This tedious operation required skill, and it was costly. It was abandoned when the pottery business became more competitive in the mid-1800s. Patterns could be stamped in the wet clay. If the stamp was dipped in blue before application, the outline would be colored. Except for impressing names, this technique also faded out around the 1850s.

Now, the wet vessel was allowed to dry to a fragile, brittle, unfired stage known as greenware. Slip, ceramic clay thinned to a liquefied state with solution, was used as a wash inside the stoneware.

By the beginning of the nineteenth century, most of the pottery produced in the United States had brown or black Albany slip linings. The clay was mined from the Hudson River area near the city that gave it its name. Glaze painting seemed to be the easiest, most rapid form of decorating, and it was applied to the surface of the delicate greenware. A brush made the decorative strokes. Or a slip cup, a container for glaze with a porcupine quill sticking out of it, might be employed to add the cobalt blue designs.

After enough decorated greenware had accumulated, it was time to fire the ware in a thickly lined, brick, underground oven. Since the firing process took six to eight days, labor costs to supervise the operation continuously were high. Because of this, the woodburning kiln (oven) was filled to capacity. Hundreds of vessels were stacked in neat rows on tiles, one on top of the other. The heat was increased gradually for a couple of days until it reached 2300 degrees Fahrenheit. At this point, the kiln was opened at the top and about a bushel of rock salt was tossed in. The oven was closed quickly, and the salt vaporized to unite with the silica in the stoneware. This formed a hard, glossy surface. If particles of salt hit the clay, some pitting resulted. The high heat was maintained for three or four days. After that, the kiln was allowed to cool gradually until the finished product could be removed.

This process was tricky because the vessels could be ruined by unsteady firing or the collapsing of the stacks. The entire cycle from clay to crock was completed in seven to ten days. There were skilled potters in various locales, but one city is especially remembered.

"It's a Bennington," a collector of stoneware may say proudly. The novice may ask, "What's a Bennington?" It's ceramic ware — anything made of clay — signed or documented by one of the two potteries that operated in Bennington, Vermont, in the 1800s. They produced over a dozen kinds of quality pottery and porcelain. Their efforts encompassed everything from Parian unglazed porcelain with a white marble look, to pipkins (small, handled pots). Candlesticks, lamps, tiles, snuff and tobacco boxes, curtain tiebacks, drawer pulls, doorknobs, vases, perfume bottles, trinket boxes, inkstands, birds, animals, whistles, bowls, washbasins, and fancy blue and white articles with a Wedgwood appearance could be included. This, however, is a book concerned with country and folk-type objects so Bennington stoneware crocks, jugs, and jars are highlighted. The Nortons and the Fentons both were located in this Vermont city.

Generally speaking, the Nortons, through various generations, were concerned with useful objects such as crocks, jars, plates, jugs, bowls, pitchers, and other household items. In 1783, eight years before Vermont's statehood, Captain John Norton established a pottery that was carried on by the family for over one hundred and one years.

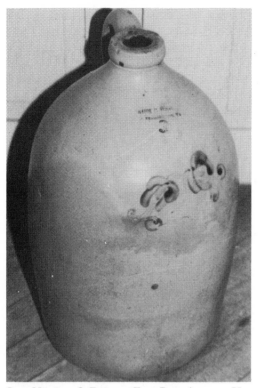

Jug, Norton & Fenton, East Bennington, Vt., 1845–1847, **$275.** Vermont.

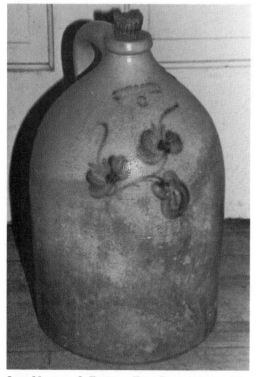

Jug, Norton & Fenton, East Bennington, Vt., 1845–1847, **$250.** Vermont.

When Christopher Webber Fenton married the captain's granddaughter, he joined the firm briefly. The partnership, named Norton and Fenton, lasted from 1845 to 1847. Christopher liked decorative articles. While he was with the firm, a few experimental wares were marketed. In 1754, Rockingham pottery, imitating that made in England with its dark mottled glaze or solid, somber color appeared. But the Norton line remained staunchly dedicated to primarily functional usage.

It was only natural that Fenton should go off on his own in 1847. He founded a company that lasted until 1859, when financial problems led to its closure. He patented some of his innovations and introduced Parian to the United States. It was Fenton who produced a Wedgwood-type, blue-and-white porcelain, emulating that made in England. Pottery and porcelain, while both made of clay, do differ. Pottery is opaque (does not let light through). Porcelain lets light through in a diffused way. Fenton's contributions to the industry were artistic.

While the Nortons' works are generally well marked, only about one-fifth of Fenton's are. Richard Carter Barret's book, *Bennington Pottery and Porcelain,* Crown Publishers, Inc., New York, 1958, contains a chart of Norton marks and the dates each was used. It is thus possible to tell that a piece marked Julius Norton, Bennington, Vt. was made between 1847 and 1850. It may help you place a date range on your stoneware. Other sources carry a similar list.

Pottery shapes help indicate age. Generally, ovoid (pear-shaped) containers were produced from about 1790 through the 1830s. Their curves were esthetically pleasing, but their narrow bottoms caused them to tip over easily. This could result in breakage, or the contents could spill out. Gradually, by the

1860s, bottoms became wider, sides flatter, and rims heavier so they were less apt to chip. Crocks had straight sides while jugs were cylindrical. In the last decade of the 1800s, undecorated, mass-produced wares prevailed, and molded merchandise was available.

In addition to this, Mason glass jars were patented in 1858, and farmwives could can their garden produce in lightweight, safe containers. Other innovations in glassmaking offered inexpensive products to the masses. Ice refrigerators and special refrigerated railroad cars to transport foods reduced the need for housewives to preserve their own vegetables, fruits, and meats. As the century turned, the salt-glazed, handmade stoneware industry faded out of existence.

Today, there is a museum in Bennington where Norton and Fenton products are attractively displayed. Other historical objects are featured, and a Grandma Moses room displays her paintings of the horse and buggy era. Children have a special area of their own where they can touch objects from the past. It is a delightful experience to take a trip back in time in Bennington.

Butter churn, Norton & Fenton, East Bennington, Vt., 1845–1847, **$150.** Vermont.

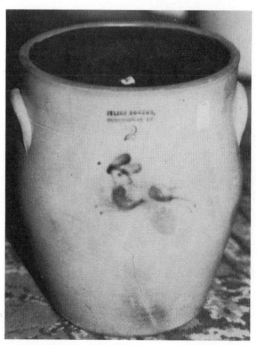

Ovoid crock, Julius Norton, Bennington, 1847–1850, **$450.** Vermont.

Ovoid jar, lid missing, L. Norton & Son, Bennington, 1833–1840, **$125.** Vermont.

Crock, E. & L. P. Norton, Bennington, Vt., 1861–1881, **$400.** Vermont.

L. Norton & Son ovoid jug, 1833–1840, **$150.** Vermont.

Ovoid crock, L. Norton, Bennington, 1828–1833, **$300.** Vermont.

Jug, J. & E. Norton, Bennington, Vt.,
1850–1859, **$275.** Vermont.

Jug, E. & L. P. Norton, Bennington, Vt.,
1861–1881, **$350.** Vermont.

Jug, J. Norton & Co., Bennington, Vt.,
1859–1861, **$250.** Vermont.

Crock, E. & L. P. Norton, Bennington, Vt.,
1861–1881, **$250.** Vermont.

Jug, E. & L. P. Norton, 1861–1881, **$275.**
Vermont.

Jug, E. Norton & Co., Bennington, Vt.,
1883–1894, **$225.** Vermont.

Jug, E. & L. P. Norton, Bennington, Vt.,
1861–1881, **$200.** Iowa.

Butter churn, E. Norton & Co., Bennington,
Vt., 1883–1894, **$125.** Vermont.

Left to right: Jug, E. & L. P. Norton, Bennington, Vt., 1861–1881, **$100.** E. Norton & Co. jug, 1883–1894, **$70.** Unmarked pitcher, 1½ gallon, **$65.** Connecticut.

6 Casual country home decor

Casual country kitchens represent the current interior designing trend in many homes. Fortunately, the desire to retrieve and revive heritage and historical articles does not include reverting to the old well or a pump to secure a supply of water. Today's kitchen faucets with their hot and cold running water are too convenient.

Back in days gone by, water did have to be hauled in, and this meant special furnishings were required. Frequently, on the back porch or in a small entryway, there was

Pine and cherry wash bench, 52″ wide, 20″ deep, 18½″ high, **$165.** Illinois.

Wash bench, hardwood top, splayed oak legs extending through top and wedged, 32″ wide, 11½″ deep, 15″ high, **$85.** Wisconsin.

Water bench, 43½″ wide, 15″ deep, 25½″ high, **$350.** Illinois.

Wainscot dry sink, 45″ wide, 18″ deep, 32″ high, 7″ splash back, **$525.** Indiana.

Dry sink, zinc lined, 51″ wide, 20″ deep, 46″ high, **$625.** Illinois.

a special place where a farmer and his hired man, in from the fields for dinner, could wash up. A bench held buckets and washbasins. A coarse towel sewed together at the ends rolled around on a circular holder so that, hopefully, a clean, dry spot could be pulled to the fore as needed. The towel couldn't fall off the rack. It was always there after you sloshed your face with soap and water with your hands, rinsed in like manner, and groped for it with your eyes squinched against a possible drip of stinging suds.

Benches also were used to hold the tubs on washday. Each Monday, dirty clothes steamed in boiling water, and rub-a-dubbing stained spots on a corrugated washboard was a common practice.

Other water needs included the dry sink, usually zinc lined, where vegetables and fruits could be prepared or dishes could be washed. It is said that the slurring of the word zinc produced the name sink.

The bedchambers had their own in-room washing facilities. A simple table with a shelf beneath could hold the chamber set that consisted of pitchers, bowl, toothbrush cup, soap dish, and the lidded slop pot to carry out waste wash water. Some tables had bars at the sides to hold towels, or were designed with a hole in the top in which the basin was set to keep it stationary. Generations ago, these were termed common washstands.

A commode washstand, which was a combination of drawers and doors, was more elaborate and provided storage space for toilet articles. Some had lift lids to accommodate the bowl and pitcher within. Frequently, the wet bottoms of these objects left rings on the shelves. A bureau commode was a small chest of drawers, with or without towel bars, and held the cleansing supplies.

Dry sink, original zinc lining (notice how the sink was cut out at the right side to fit a special place in the house), 30" wide, 20" deep, 29" high, **$450.** Illinois.

Washstand with square nails, circa 1850, 29¼" wide, 17¾" deep, 28¾" high, **$165.** Maryland.

Pine splashback washstand, early 1800s, hole for bowl in top, corner shelves for holding soap or candlesticks, 18″ wide, 16″ deep, 28½″ high, **$175.** Connecticut.

Pine washstand, 17″ wide, 13¾″ deep, 30″ high, splashback 3¾″, **$210.** Maryland.

Built-in cupboards were not the norm. Housewives of the past stored up the summer's bright fruits by simmering them with sugar until they thickened into bumpy jams. If the juices alone were cooked, the clear, shimmering results were apple yellow, strawberry red, and grape purple jellies. The kettle contents were packed in glass jars, sealed with a layer of waxy paraffin (after about 1860), and covered with a lid to keep off dust. These containers were stored by the dozens in various small cupboards that were referred to as jelly cupboards.

Because rodents and flies are attracted to sweets, the housewife kept the pies she baked in the pie cupboard. It had punched tin panels. A tin sheet was pierced full of holes by pounding a nail through it to form patterns. This permitted air to circulate to deter molding, yet prevented sharp mice teeth from gnawing through to steal bites from the pastry. Buzzing flies were not admitted either. Since the food was protected, these storage units were called pie safes. Another variety had screens on the doors and sides. If the tin wore out, it might be replaced by screening.

Other cupboards held tablewares and utensils, their contents depending on the wealth or needs of their owners. Many refer to those with wooden panels and no glass as closed cupboards. It is called step-back when its base is deeper than the top, which thus sits back a step.

When a family was wealthy enough to own plates made of pewter instead of wood, these wares were displayed in doorless cupboards with supporting rails on the shelves. These are generally spoken of as pewter cupboards.

Corner cupboards, as the name implies, were little Jack Horners and sat in the corner. This seems like a practical spacesaver , but in modern homes it may

Pine washstand, 27″ wide, 16″ deep, 27½″ high, splashback 4¼″, **$255.** Iowa.

Pine lift-top commode, 29″ wide, 17″ deep, 30″ high, **$275.** Ohio.

Pine commode washstand, origin Vermont, 29″ wide, 14½″ deep, 28″ high, splashback 3½″, **$350.** Pennsylvania.

Pine chimney cupboard, 25½″ wide, 13¼″ deep, 60¼″ high, **$325.** Georgia.

127

Jelly cupboard, original gray paint, rosehead nails, 44½" wide, 18½" deep, 56½" high, **$550.** Connecticut.

Pine pie safe with punched diamond, leaf design tin panels, 40" wide, 17¼" deep, 54" high, **$450.** Pennsylvania.

Jelly cupboard, drawers with rabbet joints and square nails, 43½" wide, 16½" deep, 49" high, **$410.** Iowa.

Pie safe with screen panels, origin South Carolina low country, 44½" wide, 19½" deep, 65½" high, **$550.** Georgia.

128

not be. Electrical wiring, windows and doors, heat registers, and other obstacles may prevent them from being backed docilely into a triangular space. They can be just too big for the area selected to confine them.

Oftentimes, a small, narrow storage unit was placed near the fireplace to hold the cooking utensils or hearth essentials. It was appropriately termed a chimney cupboard. Usually, it was rustic in appearance as if it had been knocked together to serve a purpose. Compare the two on page 132. One fits the above description, but the other has a finished look with hand-planed, molded panels on the base door. Originally, the top door was entirely of wood to match the base, but glass has been inserted. The owner has retained the panels so that the authentic qualities of the piece are maintained. This cupboard was retrieved from a farmhouse.

A Connecticut dealer attended a church auction. An extremely elderly parishioner donated a strange box-shaped item that she had neatly modernized by sticking marbleized paper on it. Not too many people were attracted to this castoff. The dealer realized it was a dough tray in which the large amounts of yeast dough required to bake a family's bread supply were mixed and allowed to rise. Some originally had legs, but often legs are added to portable versions to form tables. The example shown has irregular pegs, almost squarish, which were cut by hand. Such pegs protrude as they dry out and thus are no longer flush with the surface. This is a sign of age that antiquers treasure.

Hotels of old were called taverns. While it was possible to purchase intoxicating beverages, these taverns were not drinking establishments as such. They offered meals and sleeping accommodations to travelers. There were no private rooms listed. Male patrons, sleeping three in a bed, were piled in with strangers, while more men slept and snored on the floor. Women rarely journeyed or were accepted, but if they were, their rooms were isolated and shared with other females or children. A three-legged table with splayed (slanting out) legs and wide boards on its top is reminiscent of these tavern-time days.

The box seat with a hinged lid was a spacesaver storage area. Its back flipped down to form a table. It has multinames. It is a chair table when only one person can sit in it, a settle since its high back protected the user from drafts, or a hutch table because its seat opens to provide storage. The two pegs that lock the back in place when it is put down to form a table and the two pegs that serve as hinges are not the originals. They have been replaced. This piece, found in Georgia, is from the mid-1800s, although some bear a 1700 date.

Dough box on platform, 43″ wide, 19½″ deep, 27½″ high, **$650.** Connecticut.

Pine chair-table, top 49½" × 43½", 28" high, **$1,150.** South Carolina.

Pine step-back cupboard, two pieces, 43½" wide, 18½" deep, 33½" to step-back, 86½" overall height, **$750.** Pennsylvania.

Pine step-back cupboard, late 1800s, 35½" wide, 25½" deep at base, 33" to step-back, 68" overall height, **$750.** South Carolina.

Poplar closed cupboard, some replaced parts, 39½" wide, 18½" deep, 69" high, **$650.** Ohio.

Step-back closed cupboard, origin Madison County, Georgia, 36¼″ wide, 18″ deep, 69½″ high, **$750.** Georgia.

Pine corner cupboard with walnut trim on door panels, 39″ wide, 21″ deep, 85″ high, **$1,500.** Alabama.

Pewter cupboard, origin Georgia, 35″ wide, 11½″ deep at base, 8½″ deep at top, 84¼″ high, **$785.** Alabama.

Corner cupboard, 59½″ wide, 15″ deep, 93½″ high, **$1,600.** Georgia.

Pine corner cupboard, 25″ wide, 24″ deep, 75″ high, **$1,325.** Illinois.

Pine chimney cupboard, 26″ wide, 11½″ deep, 75″ high, **$450.** Illinois.

Pine chimney cupboard, 23″ wide, 13½″ deep, 58½″ high, **$250.** Illinois.

Pie safe with punched circle, diamond tin panels, 35½″ wide, 17½″ deep, 72″ high, **$395.** Illinois.

Note the highchair — it's a one-of-a-kind. The sixty-five-dollar boy rag doll resembles a Jack-in-the-pulpit. The high back and the "wings" by his head and arms keep off chilly drafts, and the child has his own space heater. A portable foot warmer peeks out at the lad's feet. When the heater was filled with glowing coals from the fireplace, the small holes drilled in the wooden footrest allowed the child to feel the heat. The door was closed to help retain the warmth. Small wooden wheels permit mobility. The table portion pulls out so the boy can be placed on the seat or removed. A proud grandpa probably designed and built this highchair for his first grandchild. It is too rare to price as the cost would be excessive. It is not for sale.

In the main, pioneer families sat on stools. Maybe, there was one chair for an older person or a special guest. Af-

Highchair, butterfly hinges on door, wooden rollers, holes above footrest for heat to rise from footwarmer on bottom shelf; one of a kind, no price available. Iowa.

Pie safe with punched circle tin panels, 36″ wide, 14½″ deep, 60″ high, **$395.** Georgia.

Table with pegged legs, 26½″ × 25″, 29″ high, **$85.** Checkerboard, **$87.** Rush bottom chairs, **$47.50** each. Georgia.

133

Bow-back chair, 32″ high, **$85.** Illinois.

ter the 1820s, factories produced chairs in quantities.

Rockers, much to the derision of Europeans who expected them to fall over backwards, have been an American favorite since the late 1700s. They acquire names by their style (Windsor and Boston, for example), or their uses. If Grandma peeled apples for pie while seated in one, it was her rocker from then on. It became a sewing rocker if someone sat on it to sew; or when a mother cared for her babies, it was dubbed a nursing rocker. Stout, sturdy versions were male related. Children's styles were petite.

When legs were added to a box, the desk evolved. At first, a lift lid over a storage unit was fine. Eventually, someone decided it was too much trouble to clear the top every time something was

Vermont plank-bottom chair, circa 1840, 33″ high, **$49.** Pennsylvania.

Sewing type rocker in pine, 35″ high, **$185.** Indiana.

placed inside or extracted. As a result, other types of desks were designed, and drawers filled out the leg area. Bookshelves might be added above as the desk became a handy piece of furniture for the scholar, writer, or bookkeeper.

When someone mentions a rope bedstead, it is a reference to the vertical and horizontal rope lacings that crossed and recrossed around nublike holders on the frame. This network supported the feather bed, a ticking full of feathers, which was an early type of mattress into which a person sank.

At the end of the bed shown stands a meal bin, a kitchen item. Normally, it had several compartments where bread-baking ingredients such as rye, wheat flour, or cornmeal were kept. Chests of drawers weren't necessarily used in bedrooms of yesteryear as they are today, so there have been switches from original uses by those who seek to lend a country appearance to their homes.

An easy wooden box for an inexperienced worker to pound together was a six-board chest. The bottom, hinged top, and four sides where butted together. Butted means to fasten together by putting the ends right up against each other. This is the simplest way to join two boards. Chests, trunks, and boxes made this way have many serviceable aspects.

Spinning wheels were a part of almost every household back in the days before factories produced cloth and gradually supplanted the home industry. A child's wheel that actually operates is unusual. A special feature is a leg that adjusts so that either a right- or a left-handed person could operate it.

Small units where the woman sat as she worked frequently are referred to as flax wheels because flax is a tough fiber

Child's rush-seat chair, maple and tiger maple, 29″ high, **$145.** Alabama.

Rope bedstead, maple, 52″ wide, 76″ long, 60″ high, **$800.** Meal bin, lift lid, 42″ wide, 17″ deep, 34″ high, **$495.** Ohio.

Child's rocker, jute woven seat, 15″ arm to arm, 24½″ high, **$98.** Alabama.

and both the hands and feet seemed to be required to spin it into thread. A woman walked miles and miles when she operated a large wheel, turning it with one hand as she managed the fiber with her other one. Making cloth was time consuming and energy absorbing.

This is being revived in homes today as a fascinating hobby. It sends women off to search for herbs, roots, bark, weeds, and flowers to prepare for dye; or to seek sources for freshly sheared wool to clean, comb, and spin into homespun fabrics. Wheels that are not put to work add interest to a rustic atmosphere. That's one of the appealing aspects of "going country." A home acquires a unique aura all its own.

Walnut and poplar desk, slant, lift lid, 32″ wide, 20″ deep, 51¼″ high, **$375.** Ohio.

Rocking chair, 23½″ arm to arm, 42½″ high, **$145.** Pennsylvania.

Desk, one piece, lift lid, 27″ wide, 28″ deep, 49½″ high, **$495.** Illinois.

Country secretary desk, two pieces, remnants of red paint visible, 40″ wide, 28″ deep, 29″ high at base; 35½″ wide, 13″ deep, 37½″ high at top, **$410.** Illinois.

Millwright's desk, 1¼″ thick pine, originally may have had lift lid, 40¼″ wide, 20½″ deep, 47″ high, **$450.** Virginia.

Pine country cupboard, circa 1840, 24″ wide, 18¾″ deep, 28″ high, **$375.** South Carolina.

Pine chest of drawers, 41″ wide, 18½″ deep, 30″ high, **$500.** Alabama.

Six-board chest, circa 1855, origin Lexington County, South Carolina, 36″ wide, 14″ deep, 16″ high, **$290.** South Carolina.

Bolt cabinet, 28″ wide, 11″ deep, 36″ high, **$265.** Schoenhut dolls and animals on top of cabinet, **$85** to **$100.** Iowa.

Spinning wheel, 38″ high, **$425.** Pennsylvania.

Pine trunk, 40″ wide, 19″ deep, 17½″ high, **$225.** Illinois.

Trunk for small personal possessions, 19″ wide, 12″ deep, 11″ high, **$135.** Illinois.

Child's spinning wheel, original paint,
28½″ long, 26″ high, **$500.** Ohio.

7 Pampering that precious old paint

S top! Think a moment. Do you really want to strip that commode, table, cradle, or cupboard down to the bare wood? If you do, you possibly might sing "There goes value down the drain" as you work. Certainly, a purist who is dedicated to keeping articles the way they originally were would save that finish.

One dealer asks potential customers before their proposed purchases, "Are you going to skin it?" If the reply is yes, that they do plan to splash on paint remover, then there is no sale. This dealer treasures the faded paints of the past and preserves them with a passion.

Beware! Since various country magazines have been featuring rustic painted furniture in faded blues and reds, questionable pieces are appearing. That fact was obvious when the authors of this book recently logged over eight thousand miles while on two research-photographing tours. They inspected rustic furniture made of old barn boards and knocked together in a rough manner. The results resembled the work of an amateur from the past, a man untrained in carpentry, who created a cupboard his wife needed. An "antique" paint job is no problem to fake. It is possible to buy mixes for milk-based paints or to stir together powdered milk, water, and a selected dry color purchased from an art supply store, until they form the proper consistency and tone required. This means a buyer must peruse pieces with precision before tendering a premium price. Notice! Are there forbidden runs on the back? On a split board, are there signs of paint in the crevice? These may indicate a fresh coat of fake "old paint." The people who are producing or redoing rustic furniture realize that worn spots should surround handles, pulls, and clasps that were touched constantly. They've managed to reproduce age signs in the proper places, but with the passage of time, old paint flakes off because the oils dry out. New paint

Half-round table, old blue and red paint, circa 1824, 36″ wide, 20″ deep, 28″ high, **$525**. Rag dolls range from **$85** to **$95**. Iowa.

curls off. To ascertain this would necessitate scraping the surface with a knife, and what dealer would condone such an inspection? Do observe caution in your selections.

It's always fun to find dated and signed furniture. A half-round table with soft red and blue paint has this inscription on the underside, "This table was used by Great Grandmother Hannah

Closed step-back cupboard, one piece, blue paint, New England origin, 32″ wide, 18½″ deep at base, 12¼″ deep at top, 72¾″ high, **$600.** Ohio.

in 1824 to eat her wedding breakfast on.'' A collection of rag dolls is displayed on the heirloom's top.

Actually, painted furniture dates back to colonial times (the 1600s). Chests wore coats of solid or varicolored hues. Chairs were constructed from a combination of woods, each selected for a purpose. Ash, beech, birch, or hickory were steamed and molded to form bent parts, while turnings were fashioned from ash, beech, birch, maple, and oak. Soft birch or pine could be scooped out to form seats. Paint was applied to cover up this mixture. A favorite selection was green with black, red, yellow, or brown running close behind. Painted pieces from the early- to mid-1800s are well received currently.

Thomas Sheraton (1751-1806) was a cabinetmaker who influenced styles in his native England from about 1790 through the early 1800s. His ideas reached America about 1795. If an American man saw a fine table in a city setting, he might order a copy from a

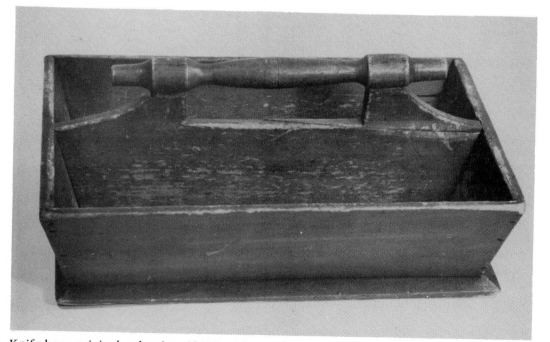

Knife box, original red paint, 12¼″ wide, 8″ deep, 5½″ high, **$65.** Illinois.

Step-back cupboard with pie shelf, base wood walnut, blue paint with a dark blue original undercoat, circa 1850, origin Indiana, 50″ wide, 19½″ deep at base, 11″ deep at top, 85½″ high, **$1,200.** Ohio.

Step-back pewter cupboard, brownish red paint, circa mid-1800s, origin North Carolina, 34″ wide, 15″ deep at base, 8½″ deep at top, 77½″ high, **$1,250.** South Carolina.

Commode washstand, black paint except for drawer front and door panel, 31″ wide, 16½″ deep, 28½″ high, 3½″ splashback, **$395.** New York.

Bucket, wooden staves, original red paint, origin Maine, 12″ diameter, 11½″ high, **$57.** Wisconsin.

country cabinetmaker who built furniture on a custom basis for customers. Thus, there are pieces with a Sheraton feel that were produced in rural sections. Families who could afford it sent their daughters to boarding schools, which were called academies or female seminaries. There studies encompassed academic subjects as well as fancy sewing. In New England especially, classes were offered in art, and a man might secure a table, stand, or box for his daughter to enhance with painted motifs including baskets of colorful fruit or flowers, scenes, or scrolls. This idea prevailed after the 1800s began until into the 1820s; and signed, dated examples of schoolgirl efforts have been preserved. How proud a family must have been to show off a daughter's ladylike skill. More pieces were decorated professionally, however.

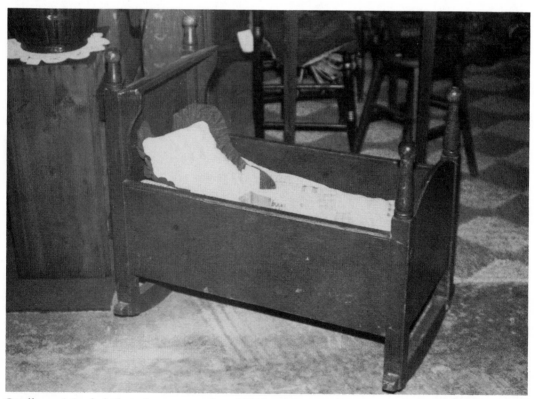

Cradle, original dark red spatter paint, 31¼″ wide, 17″ deep, 29½″ high, **$295.** South Carolina.

144

By the 1850s and on into the 1890s, furniture factories mass-produced cottage suites. Smaller sets could be purchased, but those with a bed, chairs, commode washstand, chest of drawers, rocker, standing towel rack (at times called a towel horse), and a table were available. Pine or poplar were frequently the base woods over which designs often were painted. With today's tendency to strip off paints from the past, many of these artistic efforts succumbed under the paint remover solution's action. A form of folk art flowed down the drain, and the plain pine stood skinned, ready for a new finish.

A stencil is a thin sheet of paper or metal with designs or letters cut through so that when ink or paint is applied over it, the pattern is left on the surface beneath. Stencils appeared in the United States in about 1815. Since a design or letters could be made more rapidly and accurately with their aid than by freehand painting, they were accepted eagerly.

One man who helped popularize the use of stencils to decorate wood was Lambert Hitchcock. He began making small, fancy side chairs in 1818, and established a factory in the 1820s that introduced mass production to the furniture manufacturing industry.

After a chair was completed, a paper stencil was placed on the rails and seat so that metallic powders could be applied with a pad. It took several stencils and various colors to create a vivid design that could have freehand additions as well. Seats could be plank (solid wood), rush, or cane. Many were shipped or peddled knocked down (all apart) because it took less space to transport a bundle of legs or flat slats than completed chairs.

When others saw how well Hitchcock's chairs were received, they copied

Dressing table, country Sheraton influence, stenciled and hand-painted in mustard base, origin New England, 32″ wide, 15½″ deep, 29½″ high, 5″ splashback, **$500.** Iowa.

Nightstand, base color gray with original stenciled decoration yellow and green, early 1800s, origin New York, 16¾″ wide, 15¾″ deep, 30¼″ high, 3½″ splashback, **$245.** Ohio.

145

Cottage dresser, brush and comb grained, freehand designs on drawer centers and hand-painted decorations on drawers to simulate moldings, 38½″ wide, 17″ deep, 35½″ high, **$350.** Illinois.

Lift-top cottage commode, brush and comb grained, freehand designs on top panel and door, dark lines and borders done with templates, 29″ wide, 18″ deep, 30″ high, **$375.** Illinois.

Domed pine box, New England stenciled decoration, early 1800s; repainted mid-1800s, no paint or design on back, 30″ wide, 14″ deep, 11½″ high, **$700.** Ohio.

his styles. The Hitchcock name, however, is the generic (family) title assigned to all of them. His are marked with a stencil on the back of the seat frame. From 1825–1829, it read "L. Hitchcock, Hitchcocks-ville, Conn. Warranted." In the 1829–1843 period during a partnership with Arba Alford, Jr., a relative by marriage, the mark was "Hitchcock, Alford, & Co., Hitchcocks-ville, Conn. Warranted." From 1820–1852, it returned to his name with a new town, and read, "Lambert Hitchcock, Unionville, Conn."

Even though the designs may be well worn from constant contact with generations of sitters, it is suggested that the patterns should be retained and not stripped off. Labels help date and authenticate antiques. They should always be preserved.

Examine the two lift-top commodes on page 150. They are similar, but what is their main difference? One has been artificially grained while the other is made from the wood of the chestnut tree. That's what graining can do — imitate another rarer and, usually, more expensive wood.

Graining was utilized in this country in the 1600s, and continued to be featured in the latter part of the 1800s. The authors' observations and tips received through consultation with two artists who are familiar with graining devices and skills helped in the analysis of the patterns on various pieces of furniture.

It should be kept in mind that there are two possible approaches. The selected applicator could be moved over a wet surface to stroke, dab, or swirl on designs. Conversely, the applicator itself could be wet and could be moved across a dry surface as desired to create designs. This means that it was possible to achieve a wide range of patterns and colors, especially if a piece of furniture had

Stenciled chair, 29½" high, **$65.** Iowa.

Stenciled chair, 30" high, **$75.** Connecticut.

147

Child's stenciled rocker, **$135.** Alabama.

Boston rocker, stenciled, 41¼″ high, **$250.** Connecticut.

Cane seat stenciled rocker, signed "C. Rodinson, R. I." is 36″ high, **$150.** Illinois.

Child's cane seat and back rocker, gold stenciled, circa 1860, 14½″ arm to arm, 25¼″ high, **$200.** Iowa.

an already dry, painted base, over which to work.

Tools also differed. A narrow comb with elongated teeth and a widened base to assure a good hand grip was employed frequently. The comb might have been made of cork, metal, or from gutta-percha, a rubber-like gum secured from certain trees found in Southeast Asia. Then again, an amateur could create his own comb from cardboard or wood and vary the width, the number of teeth, and perhaps the spaces between the prongs.

The simplest use of the combing technique can be seen in the match safe and candle shelf where fine teeth have produced narrow lines that are stroked on. The outside designs, on the border of the candle sconce, are produced through dabbing, perhaps with the aid of a piece of cardboard or cloth. The initials on the match safe are trailed on with a fingertip.

Match safe, comb grained, initials done with finger, 4½″ wide, 11½″ high, **$52.** Ohio.

A similar graining pattern can be seen on the hooded cradle. The vertical lines were combed on and allowed to dry. The sweeping dark pigment crossing the grain is an example of freehand wet brushing to break the monotony of the precise combing.

Interesting results can be produced with a sponge. The blanket chest was first coated with a light base color and allowed to dry. The dark design was achieved by permitting pigment to seep into a sponge that was then pressed against the wood at regular intervals. The depth of the darkness depended on the degree of saturation of the sponge. The designs achieved are as individual as the artist, and careful workmanship, but not much artistic skill is required to use this method.

It is not advisable or wise to state unequivocally that the graining on a par-

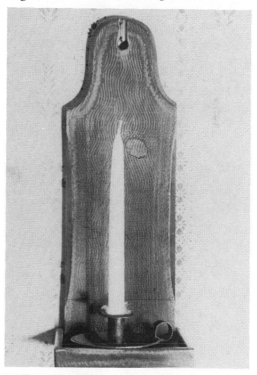

Wall candle sconce, comb-grained wood, 7″ wide, 5½″ deep, 18″ high, **$175.** Illinois.

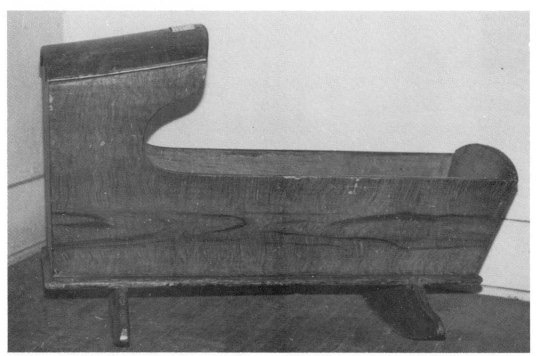

Cradle, comb grained with freehand horizontal brushstrokes, 39″ long, 14″ wide, 23½″ high, **$395.** Iowa.

Chestnut lift-top commode, 30″ wide, 17″ deep, 31½″ high, **$325.** Pennsylvania.

Lift-top commode, brush and comb graining, 30¼″ wide, 16¼″ deep, 32″ high, **$375.** Connecticut.

Dovetailed blanket chest, mustard base paint, dark sponged designs, 41″ wide, 20″ deep, 25″ high, **$275.** Ohio.

Grained box with feather, brush, or comb graining and cloth dabbed near lock area to achieve dark vertical pattern, 20″ wide, 12″ deep, 6″ high, **$285.** Georgia.

ticular piece resulted from the use of a single tool or method. In many cases, a similar effect could be produced through the use of various tools, or a pattern was achieved by combining several methods, as with the cradle already discussed with its combed and brushed coating. Sometimes, it would be impossible to say what tool was used because artists often developed their own preferences.

The small box is an example of graining that could have been achieved by using a dry brush, a comb, a feather, or some unknown device. First, a light base coat was applied. When it was dry, darker pigment was stroked over the piece and dry brushed to pick up the excess pigment. Similarly, a feather could have performed this function, as could a comb in conjunction with a dry brush.

To complete the design, a rag was dabbed on the surface where some wet color remained to achieve the central vertical grain. A pooling effect can be seen where excess pigment accumulated to form the dense lines or strokes.

A brush was used on the next three pieces. Simple strokes on the flat surfaces of the washstand emulate an artificial grain. Freehand brushing with a semi-dry brush is in evidence on the cupboard. As the strokes neared the base of the doors, the amount of pigment remaining on the brush gradually diminished. Lastly, on the face of the blanket chest, the sweeping brush-strokes of the artist can readily be seen. The effect was accomplished by a wet application of pigment followed by dry brushing to remove the excess color.

Cloths were used extensively by artists to develop designs on furniture. Their shapes varied, but generally a piece of

Common washstand, artificially grained by freehand brushing, 28″ wide, 16″ deep, 30″ high, 5¼″ splashback, **$200.** Alabama.

Cupboard, artificially grained by freehand brushing dark pigment over dry base, 33½″ wide, 12″ deep, 57″ high, **$400.** Illinois.

Blanket chest with German fraktur dated 1811 inside lid, two drawers at base, dovetailed, turned feet, gold stenciled, artificially grained by freehand, sweeping brush strokes, circa 1826, 46″ wide, 23″ deep, 28″ high, **$1,800.** Two youth Windsor chairs flanking blanket chest, 30¾″ high, **$300** each. Ohio.

Samuel Bauman,
Drucker zu
Ephrata.
1811.

Close-up of dated area on fraktur.

Stenciled butter churn, 14″ wide, 14″ deep, 35″ high, **$195.** Illinois.

Anvil on red painted and stenciled wooden base with hand-forged tongs, 11″ wide, 11″ deep, 30½″ high, **$125.** Illinois.

cloth was shaped to fit the hand, and then excess pigment was removed by wiping the surface. The rags had to be kept dry, so clean ones had to be available. Conversely, a pattern could be attained by dabbing a rolled cloth on the wet surface in order to achieve the darker center pattern. In all probability, this is how the chest of drawers was textured.

The decided markings on the leather-topped document box were probably done with a tightly folded cloth or a shaped piece of putty. These were pressed on the very wet surface to create the pronounced effect. Notice how all the vertical lines express a similarity in design. The base was probably blotted with a cloth to look mottled and flattened.

The grained, domed trunk exemplifies a cloth-wiped swirling accomplished without a desire to achieve symmetry. There are indiscriminate zigzags and whorls . . . perhaps the work of a first-time designer. In contrast, notice the apparent care that was taken in cloth wiping the hooded cradle. The design is certainly a simple one that was executed with smooth strokes by a meticulous person who wanted to be proud of his creation.

Decorating furniture is limited only by the artist's originality. Give him other graining tools such as textured leather, corncobs, crinkled paper, a graining roller, stencils, paper cards, vinegar to achieve a highly mottled effect, the smoke from a candle or a kerosene lamp — and innumerable artistic creations can result.

Chest of drawers, pattern achieved with a piece of cloth wiping off excess pigment and daubs on center designs on drawers, 41″ wide, 20¼″ deep, 46½″ high, **$550.** Ohio.

Document box with leather bands. Textured effect on wood was achieved by pressing a shaped piece of cloth on a very wet surface and then blotting the base to give a mottled effect, 19½″ wide, 9½″ deep, 8″ high, **$175.** Connecticut.

Domed lid trunk, artificially grained by wiping a dry cloth over a wet surface, 34″ wide, 21″ deep, 19″ high, **$265.** Iowa.

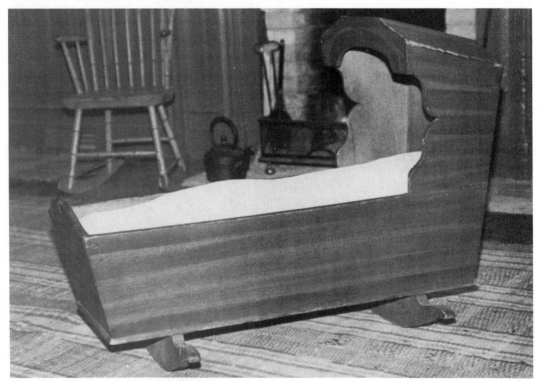

Hooded child's cradle, New England origin, green inside, artificial mahogany graining on the outside achieved by stroking wet pigment with a dry cloth, 36½″ long, 14″ wide, 28″ high, **$650.** Ohio.

8 Style influences of religious groups

No buttons, no zippers, no telephones, no electricity, no mechanical machinery, no education beyond eighth grade, no insurance, no lightning rods, no faces on dolls, horse and buggies instead of automobiles, and a patriarchal society are edicts accepted by this group. Who practices these beliefs? The Amish.

The women wear long, unadorned dresses and bonnets. The men have wide-brimmed hats and beards. The children are parted from worldly contamination because the boys are miniatures of the men in their apparel. The girls' dark dresses are well below their knees, and white, flat caps perch on their heads, distinguishing them from little girls in bright dresses, shorts, or slacks.

Members are forbidden to go to war. (Some were in the Revolution, and others fought against slavery, however.) They must not take oaths or hold public office. They meet in homes every two weeks to worship. They till the soil with the aid of horses, and simplicity of living is stressed. The Amish are a strict Protestant sect, originally part of the Mennonite (Swiss Brethren) church that developed in Switzerland in 1525 and believed in adult baptism. The Amish were stricter than other branches of the Mennonite Church, which felt evildoers should be punished by being shut off from the rite of Holy Communion. The Amish completely avoid anyone who has sinned.

Jacob Ammann, a Swiss Mennonite leader for whom the Amish are named, led them in breaking with the Mennonites in 1687. The first Amish came to America seeking religious freedom in 1728. While they have communities in twenty-three states, their largest groups are in Ohio, Pennsylvania, Indiana, Iowa, and Illinois.

A prominent Ohio dealer was asked

Amish walnut and cherry chest of drawers, dated 1895, 43½″ wide, 21″ deep, 49″ high, 5″ back rail, **$650.** Ohio.

how he knew that an article of furniture was Amish. "That's easy for me," he replied. "I buy it from the Amish."

A walnut and cherry Amish chest has an unusual drawer formation. The owner's inscribed initials, "E" for Enos, and "Y" for Yoder, and "1895" can be noted. A scribed design and a stain applied to imitate inlay show on the drawers. The drawers are joined by dovetails (resemble birds' tails and interlock like jigsaw

Close-up of Amish bedpost showing pegged construction.

puzzle pieces). The bottoms are chamfered (edges cut to slant to fit in the sides). This style was made from the mid- to late-1800s. Modern examples are made of oak and a dovetail construction is not used. Careful craftmanship of this nature is an Amish trait.

A poplar workbench has been converted for bathroom use by building up the base and cutting a hole in the top to accommodate the washbasin. The piece has plain, utilitarian lines.

An Amish cradle came from south-central Ohio. It is larger than usual so that the baby would not outgrow it too soon. There are slats in the bottom and braces have been added to help prevent tipping and to add stability. The plain lines indicate Amish ancestry.

The false graining on this single rope bed was achieved by applying off-white colors covered with exaggerated brush-strokes in stain. The off-round pegs protrude above the surface of the post

Amish rope bedstead, artificially grained, 52¼" wide, 73½" long, 39" high, circa 1840, **$200.** Iowa.

Amish poplar workbench, 49½″ wide, 20″ deep, 33″ high, **$800.** Ohio.

Amish birch cradle with oak rockers, 46″ wide, 18½″ deep, 22″ high, **$195.** Pennsylvania.

showing that the surrounding wood has dried out with age. The fat, round finials are called cannonballs. The bed was purchased near Kalona, Iowa.

Amish dolls are often called bups. They wear somber black, violet, or purple garments. Girls nine or ten years old operate treadle sewing machines so well that they can make their own toys. The dolls are faceless so that they will not appear to be graven images and displease God. Since hickory bends well, it was used to make the frame of the child's rocker. Similar rockers for adults are also available, and the style dates from the last of the 1800s until the present. Bark often adhered to the bottom of the old, solid seats that have been replaced by slat construction today.

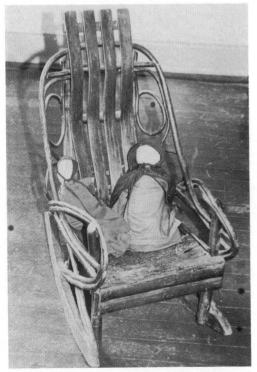

Amish child's rocker, hickory branches and plank seat, **$125.** Ohio.

An Amish boy doll, the first one the dealer ever had, was acquired after a request was made for boy toys. He rides a non-Amish horse which has an animal skin covering. Any lad could play with stuffed animals. The Amish are proud of their colorful quilts, a bright touch in drab homes, and they sell them; but they are ashamed to show the worn toys. They can't understand why anyone would want them.

The plain, sturdy Amish cupboard is unusual because the primary wood (wood that shows) is of pine. The secondary wood (not exposed), including the back and the drawer bottom, is walnut. The drawer front is butternut. The glass has the old wavy look. Green paint covers the original red, and the dealer plans to take off the outer coat with great care in order to expose the red. The wood is one and one-fourth inches thick, except for the side pieces that measure one and one-half inches.

The Amana Society

The Amana Church Society grew out of the Church of True Inspiration, founded by Eberhard Gruber and Johann Rock, who objected to the German Lutheran doctrine. They believed God revealed himself to a human instrument and thus communicated directly with man.

Church members were persecuted in Europe because they would not take legal oaths, send their children to public schools, or enroll for military service. They established communities where all shared, working together for the common good, but the persecution continued. Finally, in 1842, under Christian Metz's leadership, land was bought near Buffalo, New York, and more than eight hundred Inspirationists immigrated to seek religious freedom.

Amish stuffed toys: dog, **$55.** Camel, **$55.** Dog with ears, **$55.** Hen in front, **$35.** Iowa.

Amish boy doll, **$200.** Animal skinned rocking horse on frame, **$700.** Iowa.

Amish cupboard of pine, butternut, and walnut, with green overcoat over the original red, 48″ wide, 17¼″ deep, 84½″ high, **$850.** Iowa.

Pennsylvania Amish two-piece step-back cupboard, 43″ wide, 16½″ deep, 80½″ high, **$950.** Pennsylvania.

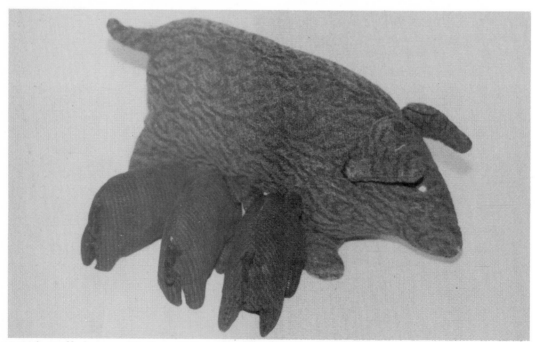

Amish stuffed sow with three little pigs: sow, 12½″ long, 6″ high; pigs 4½″ long, 3″ high, **$100** the set. Iowa.

When this location of some eight thousand acres prospered and became too crowded, the Amish migrated to Iowa in 1855 after securing eighteen thousand acres of government land for pioneer development. In the Bible, Song of Solomon 4:8, a mountain peak called Amana is mentioned. It means true, fixed, to remain faithful. This name was chosen for the new Iowa commune with its seven villages, and so the Amana Society was born.

The first Iowa village was named Amana, meaning Remain Faithful. Other nearby villages were erected by 1862 and were named by directions; for example, West Amana, South Aman, etc.

Families were assigned living quarters in houses, ate in communal kitchens, were delegated jobs, and went to church ten times a week. While living simply in farming communities, they also had a woolen works, flour mills, and brick and lumberyards. This gave them merchandise to sell to the outside world.

Sixty-seven years later, in 1932, a company was formed, stocks were distributed, and the community kitchens were closed. The communal aspect was over, but the residents remained faith-

Amana rope bedstead, cherry, mid-nineteenth century, 40″ wide, 80½″ long, 37″ high, **$425.** Iowa.

Amana pine cupboard, 38″ wide, 17½″ deep, 62½″ high, **$650.** Iowa.

Amana storage cupboard, artificially grained, mid-nineteenth century, 43½″ wide, 19″ deep, 46″ high, **$550.** Iowa.

ful to their traditions. They continue to worship on Sundays in their village meeting houses. Services originally were in German, but today they are conducted in German or English. During periods of worship, the church members wear age-honored attire. The men dress in dark suits while the women wear aprons and shawls. Black caps cover their hair.

One Amana resident stated with pride that she is the granddaughter of the first baby born in Main Amana. It is customary for all brides to have a handmade quilt, and the resident's fingers were pricked and sore from quilting the previous day for a bride-to-be in her sister's family. Since every Amana home has these coverings, the bride could not sleep without her quilt.

A walnut wall clock, a plain cupboard, and an unadorned wardrobe (closets were lacking) were expected furnishings in nineteenth century homes. While most was functional and plain, furniture that the colonists brought from their German homeland might be more ornate with paint or inlay work. Amana cabinetmakers occasionally constructed veneered, carved, or inlaid pieces. Wood was finished in natural tones, and color was lacking in the home decor.

If there was a child of two years or under, the mother and the other young children were allowed to eat at home, where only a sitting room and a bedroom were needed. They procured their food in insulated, picnic-type, covered baskets from the communal kitchen where everyone else ate. If necessary, the transported food could be warmed on the heating stove. At meals, the men, women, and children sat at separate tables, which had square, tapered legs.

Husbands and wives slept in separate beds. Reproduction was not encouraged

Amana drainboard, used to work and drain the whey out of the cheese curds when making cheese, 31″ wide, 17½″ deep, 17½″ high at back, 15½″ high at front where it drains, **$160.** Iowa.

Amana-made brass lock, 4″ square, **$95.** Iowa.

Amana-made tin serving tray, 15″ wide, 9½″ deep, **$40.** Iowa.

Bishop Hill corner cupboard, pine with walnut knob, 48″ wide, 28″ deep, 91″ high, **$795.** Illinois.

Bishop Hill pine corner cupboard, 46″ wide, 26″ deep, 48″ high, **$450.** Illinois.

since a mother was not expected to work and contribute her share in service for the good of the community when she had children under three years of age. Babies also meant more non-workers to feed because boys and girls, ages five through fourteen, attended school six days a week all year round. They did have time off to help with the harvesting of crops, however, and did knit or crochet hats, mittens, scarves, and stockings. The wife went through a period of discipline in the church after the birth of a child, and only gradually earned back her status, including her right to sit with the other women.

Each of the seven Amana villages was a self-sufficient unit with its own trained artisans. The cobbler, basketmaker, baker, butcher, harness-maker, cabinet-maker, blacksmith, and tinsmith passed their knowledge on to others. Examples of their quality workmanship still exist.

Fine, handcrafted furniture with hand-rubbed finishes is made in the Amanas currently.

Bishop Hill, Illinois

In 1846, when Jansonists(named for their preacher-leader, Eric Jansson) failed to reform the Swedish Lutheran State Church, they immigrated to America to found their Christian Utopia. By pooling their resources, they were able to pay for passage across the Atlantic, through the Erie Canal, and across the Great Lakes to Chicago. From there, the families walked one hundred and fifty miles to meet their leader at the site of what would become Bishop Hill, Illinois. They arrived in September, and one hundred of them didn't survive that first cold winter spent in hillside caves with poor sanitary facilities and little food.

When spring arrived, with a "one for all and all for one" communal spirit, the survivors tilled the soil, planted crops, and began to build shelters. In a few years, a planned village flourished on the prairie. It was not like the log cabin settlement in New Salem, Illinois, where Abraham Lincoln lived from July, 1831, through spring, 1836, or similar to the small wooden homes the colonists left behind in Sweden. Many of Bishop Hill's buildings were constructed of handmade brick in a Greek Revival style, well proportioned with classical lines and columns. There were two elaborate hotels, one with a ballroom where festive dances were held.

The settlers were not somber people. However, based on biblical teachings, there was no private property. All lands, buildings, animals, produce, and industries were owned jointly by the people. All ate together. All worked at assigned tasks. By the 1850s, Bishop Hill had become the major commercial center in west-central Illinois. Furniture produced there sold well. Eric Jansson died in 1850, but the community prospered until bad investments and bickering among members of the board of trustees caused the property to be divided. By 1861, individual ownership replaced the New Jerusalem Utopia the Swedes had hoped to establish. Today much restoration work has been completed, and members of the Swedish royal family have been guests in the village.

What sort of furniture did the colonists make? In the church, the pews of thick walnut finished with linseed oil have darkened maple spindles so symmetrical that they are in perfect alignment up and down the rows. The ancestor of the hideway bed sofa, perhaps, is a solid bench that can be transformed into a sleeping unit for two. A rocking butter churn with a lift lid in the center for pouring in cream, resembles a rocking horse without a head and tail. Native woods were used, and maple rope beds were prevalent. Two cupboards from Bishop Hill are illustrated.

The Dunkards

You may call them Dunkers (because they immersed converts in water to baptize them) or you may call them Dunkards. Properly, you should call them the Church of the Brethren. They are a sect of German-American Baptists who oppose military service and taking oaths. The first group arrived in this country in 1719 after crossing the Atlantic Ocean to avoid religious persecution in Germany. The New Testament is the basis for their strict beliefs and living patterns.

In addition to their objection to war, their plain dress and language sets them aside as non-conformists. They believe in rituals such as foot washing ceremonies and the kiss of charity. Their farms in Pennsylvania, Ohio, and Indiana prospered.

What could be a better pre-wedding gift for a bride than a friendship quilt? (See Color Section.) Friends signed and sewed it, and thus it is a cloth love token. If the script is all the same, one person wrote the names. They represent the usual Dunkard families: Miller, Brubaker, Garber, Denlinger. Mama meant Grandma, and Mother was Mom. Aunt and Uncle appear just that way. A heart square in the middle is romantic. Delicate feather-stitching was used. It is an Eaton, Ohio, "autograph book" in cloth form, signed and hand sewn by Dunkard friends. It covers a nineteenth-century pine and maple cannonball bed. Note the round finials that give the bed its name. Since this was a popular style, it cannot be attributed to the Dunkards. Interlaced rope supported the ticking-covered "mattress."

The Moravians

The Moravian Brethren originally were German Lutherans and came into existence in Bohemia and Moravia in 1457. They were inspired by the doctrines of John Huss, a man who was burned at the stake for his beliefs in 1415. Moravians were to give Christ first place in their hearts and go any place in the world in His service. They were required to pray and worship daily. They participated in footwashing ceremonies and in the kiss of peace.

In 1735 with August Gottlieb Spangenberg as their leader, they settled in Georgia, and in 1736 moved to Pennsylvania. They founded the city of Bethlehem in 1741. Spangenberg organized a semi-communistic settlement in which time and labor, but not personal property, were shared. All work was for the benefit of the church. By 1747, when their leader left for a religious assignment elsewhere, the communal organization gave way to individual enterprise. By 1753, many Moravians resided in Salem, North Carolina.

They avoided the "follies of the fashionable life," living simply and dressing in a plain manner. They provided educational facilities for their sons and daughters. At first, enrollment in their boarding schools was restricted to Moravians. Later, in the late 1700s and early 1800s, others were admitted until the Bethlehem Seminary had two thousand girls from twenty-four states registered.

Art was taught to thank God for giving them the skills required to create beauty. The young ladies' paintings and needlework creations were colorful, elaborate, and kept up with current trends.

In woodcrafts, the Moravians likewise departed from the staid furniture of other sects. While straight, structural lines were employed, the craftsmen enhanced their furniture with some painted decorations, carving, or inlay work. (See Color Section.) When pegs can be removed so that a table can be taken apart to become compact, it is easy to transport or store. Such a Moravian table probably came to the New World with the colonists. It is dated underneath, May 10, 1713, and the top is outlined with colorful inlay. There are no nails in it. There is a sliding lid and a drawer for storage. Add shoe feet, and the word's unique, because that's what this table is — unique.

The Mormons

An angel named Moroni, golden plates with peculiar writing on them, and visions inspired the formation of a new religious group in the United States. In 1827, golden plates dug out of a hillside near his home in Palmyra, New York, were translated by Joseph Smith and became the Book of Mormon. In 1830, Smith established the Church of Jesus Christ of Latter-Day Saints, but because of the book, people call the members Mormons.

Mormons believe in repentance, the trinity of God, baptism by immersion, the laying on of hands for gifts from the Holy Spirit, and the direct revelation of God through prophets. They have faith in the Bible, but also trust the Book of Mormon and other Divine revelations. They practice religious ceremonies in which deceased persons who were not of the faith can be baptized so that they can live eternally with their Mormon families. Polygamy, which some practiced, was not included in their original doctrines. Polygamy to the Mormons meant the man could have many wives. This practice later was forbidden.

Joseph Smith tried to build a New Jerusalem, but he and his followers were driven out of Missouri where they settled. In 1838, the Illinois town of Nauvoo was founded by the Mormons and flourished. When trouble flared there, Smith was arrested, and a mob attacked the jail where he was held and shot him to death. The Mormons were forced to leave Nauvoo in 1846. Amid hardships, many walked pulling handcarts or jolted in wagons across the country to establish new homes in the Valley of the Great Salt Lake, Utah, then not a part of the United States. Led by Brigham Young, they worked hard, prospered, and built a religiously oriented city.

Pictured is an artificially grained dry sink from about the middle of the nineteenth century. It came from Nauvoo. Since there was a shortage of trees in arid Utah, Young told the Mormons to pack supplies in cases made of wood that could be knocked apart to remake

Nauvoo dry sink, artificially grained, mid-nineteenth century, 48½″ wide, 24½″ deep, 36″ high at front, 45″ high at rear, **$565.** Iowa.

into furniture. At times, he used a feather to grain woodwork artificially, and he enjoyed practical pastimes of this type.

The Shakers

Rove about chanting, "Love, love." Stamp your feet to tread out evil. Wave your hands to gather blessings. These were parts of the ritualistic religious dancing of the United Society of Believers. Because of their intense, emotional, shaking movements, outsiders dubbed them Shakers. Males and females did not shuffle about together. Each remained in his or her segregated line or circle. It was said that the Hosts of Heaven worshipped in this manner.

Austerity characterized this sect that was started in England about 1706. In 1758, Ann Lee joined the society, and in 1770 she was recognized by members as the first leader of the Church of God on earth. Shakers called her Mother Ann. A group of Shakers came to America in 1774 and organized a society of Watervliet, New York.

They believed God was both male and female, and they were forbidden to marry. The sect did accept orphans, and, when families became converts, the children became part of the fold.

Work was a form of worship, and the Shakers devotedly performed their assigned duties. They invented farm implements and machinery, flat brooms, condensed milk, circular saw blades, and many other laborsaving devices. The merchandise they sold was top quality, and those who worked with wood were fine craftsmen. Women wove the seats on chairs, and sometimes different colored tapes were interlaced to form attractive patterns. They also made splint, rush, or cane seats and backs.

The society began selling chairs in the

Shaker child's rocker, size O, stenciled patent date May 14, 1878, origin Mount Lebanon, New York, 24½″ high, **$300.** Ohio.

Shaker cupboard, red paint, hand-planed doors, thumbnail molding, 35″ wide, 18″ deep, 74″ high, **$1,500.** Ohio.

1700s, and by 1850 they placed numbers on them which indicated sizes. A number "0" designated a child-size. This Mount Lebanon, New York, rocker is not typical, but does have the Shaker finish. Wood, not woven tape, forms the seat and back. It bears the date "May 14, 78," marked with a stencil.

The red Shaker cupboard stands on straight legs. It has dainty thumbnail molding, and the solid sides have the typical high scroll arches at the base. The craftsmanship indicates Shaker because the shelves differ in thickness, distance apart, and are of graduated sizes. The brothers and sisters disliked clutter. Because of this, they assigned places for objects with shelves and drawers precisely sized according to the space required.

A cluster of Shaker-related items is shown. The society sold sewing kits around the turn of the century. The box, only, is displayed, without the kit. The long wooden handle with the funnel-like tin end is a crop duster. It must have kept insects from destroying many growing plants. The top unscrews where the powder was inserted. The checkerboard is old, crudely contrived, and not of Shaker origin, but is a desirable collectible.

Two butter churns show Shaker characteristics. The first is a dasher version in a piggin style (one stave extends to form a handle). The fingers are the pointed laps of the type used by this religious group.

Shakers needed huge butter churns since all meals were served from a communal kitchen. A mate to this churn was sold at a Shaker auction, and was called a Canterbury butter churn.

Shaker furniture was clean in line and plain, without carvings or other adornment. Its excellent workmanship and

Side view of Shaker cupboard showing high scroll ends.

Shaker cardboard box for sewing kits that were sold to the public at the turn of the century, without the kit, **$32.** Shaker crop duster, tin with wooden handle, 24½″ high, **$60.** Iowa.

Shaker butter churn, piggin style, with but-
tonhole hoops around churn, 9″ diameter,
38″ high, **$225.** Iowa.

Kentucky Shaker walnut table, diamond-
shaped pegs go through the top, 36″ wide,
29″ deep, 28½″ high, **$1,000.** Iowa.

Shaker Canterbury butter churn, 15½″
wide, 26″ deep, 39½″ high, **$225.** Iowa.

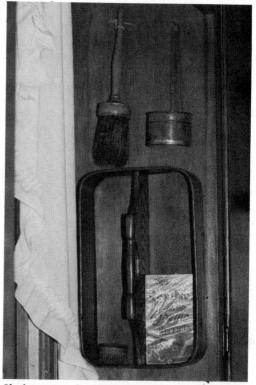

Shaker wooden handled brush, 12″ high,
$32. Tin dipper, 9″ high, **$25.** Bentwood
silverware case, 13″ wide, 8½″ deep, 2¾″
high, **$75.** Lice comb, **$32.** Cook book,
$28. Iowa.

Clothes crate used by two Shaker Sisters for carrying a load of wet laundry, 25¼ " long, case, 20″ × 20″, 9″ high, **$450.** ohio.

Shaker sap bucket, iron diamond support at top, metal bands, marked "N F Shakers, Enfield, N.H." 11¾ " diameter, 11″ high, **$90.** Iowa.

simple beauty is respected by modern homemakers who appreciate such artistry.

Zoar, Ohio

German Lutherans who sought to revive the devotional ideal in the Lutheran Church were called Pietists. When their devout religious convictions were not welcomed, they sought a refuge from persecution and established a communal colony at Zoar, Ohio, in 1817. Their leader was J. Bimeler (or Bimiler).

The group sold furniture, ironwork, and pottery outside their community. Their early works were based on solid woodworking traditions from Germany. The colony outlived its founder, but dissolved in 1898, after eighty-one years of successful existence. Most experiments in communal living have terminated much more rapidly. In 1936,

the Pietist village became a state memorial, where it is now possible to view the home of their leader and the Old Zoar Garden.

American pewter is treasured because there is not a great deal of it. Early examples are not marked "pewter." They have touch-marks that were the maker's identity symbols. Generally, it was not until the 1900s that the word "pewter" was placed on these wares.

The eight-inch-high, American pewter ejector candlestick indicates the size of the miniature walnut blanket chest. The chest was purchased at a Zoar, Ohio, auction held in May, 1980. The hand-bills indicated it was from the estate of Hilda R. Morhart, who was referred to as the "First Lady of Zoar." She knew about the community and wrote about its history. Notice the tiny triangular dovetails that interlock the sides and the front of the chest. In order to help keep

Zoar two-piece cherry cupboard, raised cross panels in doors, no guides in drawer compartments, space between base and top served as a pie shelf, 51½" wide, 19½" deep at base, 12½" deep at top, 85½" high, **$2,500.** Ohio.

Zoar walnut miniature blanket chest, 22" wide, 10½" deep, 10" high, **$450.** Indiana.

them even in size and length, scribe marks are inscribed in the walnut. The top has breadboard ends — narrow pieces of wood that are attached across the grain to help prevent warping and add strength.

"This two-piece cupboard used to be a horse," remarked the dealer who owns it. He explained that he exchanged an animal for the cupboard. The simple, unadorned lines are typical of Zoar craftsmanship. The drawer bottoms are chamfered (cut at a slant to fit in the sides). The top shelf has an arch cutout of the middle so the high-up contents can be reached more easily, a German idea. There are dovetails at the back, but machine-made nails are used at the front. The molding resembles a rain gutter because it sets out from the top. The piece is painted.

A cherry, step-back closed cupboard has raised panels which form an "X" pattern. This was frequently used, but a large, raised diamond design is a more common Zoar characteristic. The path of the hand plane can be felt on the surface where there were slight "waves." The drawers do not have guides. The cupboard dates to the early 1800s.

With the exception of the Mormons, all the religious groups discussed in this chapter came to the United States to escape religious persecution. The Mormon Church, the one native organization, was founded in New York State, yet its members knew scorn and violence. Most of the sects made furniture that had plain lines and was without ornamentation. However, the Moravians embellished theirs with inlay, carvings, and painted decorations. Each group added their skills to the production of furniture that is a part of America's heritage.

Zoar two-piece pine cupboard, origin Zoar, Ohio, 43″ wide, 21½″ deep, 85″ high, **$595.** Pennsylvania.

9 Kitchen molds

There are all sorts of kitchen molds—for bread, rice, cornmeal, cake, cookie, maple sugar, butter, cheese, pudding, candy, and ice cream to mention a few. Cooks of the past knew that food with eye appeal appeared more appetizing.

One year, a family decided to have a Dickens of a Christmas. If they were to follow Charles Dickens' storybook Tiny Tim through the holiday, it would be necessary to roast a plump goose, and, of course, a steamed plum pudding was a must for an English dinner fit enough for a Scrooge to "Bah, humbug." A search of cookbooks has failed to uncover a recipe with plums in it. Citron, raisins, and currant jelly, but not even one shriveled prune was in the list of ingredients.

Tin rice boiler mold, 8″ diameter, 7″ high, **$22.** Georgia.

In days gone by, brandy was poured over the finished pudding at serving time, ignited, and the whole dessert flamed. Instead, try encircling the pudding with lumps of sugar soaked in vanilla, lemon, or orange extract. Set a match to one cube, and a fire ring results . . . a flaming end to a feast.

It might be a little more difficult to stare at the dismayed face of a hog's head cheese mold. After most of the meat had been cared for following butchering time in the late autumn, the farm wife boiled the animal's head until the meat fell off the bones. She chopped it, added seasonings, mixed it with the broth from the cooking, and poured it into molds. It jelled when it grew cold because a gelatin came out of the bones. That's head cheese.

A woebegone cat carved in relief (raised above the surface) on a walnut board created an impression in cheese made from cream or milk. Wooden pegs distributed about on the feline's form were removed. When the mold was pushed with pressure into the soft cheese, any excess liquid drained up through the holes, but the cat image remained on top.

Tin pudding molds, left: 8½″ long, 6½″ wide, 5″ high, **$22.50.** Right: 8¾″ diameter, 5″ high, **$20.** Illinois.

Tin pudding mold, 12″ long, 6″ deep, 3¼″ high, **$65.** Iowa.

Cast iron hog's head cheese mold, 10″ diameter, **$65.** Indiana.

If you plan to make a row of plump candy Santas, a lamb, or a series of hearts, you should purchase quality chocolate, not chips, to melt and pour into molds, previously sprayed lightly with a non-sticking commercial spray. Refrigerate to harden slightly. Dip quickly in hot water and remove the candy to permit it to set until firm. Many molds originated in Germany, but others are French. Most were made of tin, but some of copper may be found. Occasionally, there may be a pewter mold. After the turn of the century, aluminum was used frequently. Older examples usually have more detailed lines, while new ones are skimpy in appearance. Genuinely old molds should look as if they have been used. It is fun to search for different forms such as Indians, a lamb, or Saint Nicholas in his flowing robe, the forerunner of jolly Santa. There are dealers who say that rows of hearts are in demand. Rabbits are abundant unless they assume uncommon poses. Animals other than bunnies add dimension to collections.

Another confection comes from a tree. Maple sap runs in the early spring. After a hole about three inches deep and four feet above the ground is bored through the bark, a spout is inserted and a bucket is hung over it to catch the sap. When enough accumulates, it is boiled to remove most of the water content until a syrup remains. A longer boiling period produces maple sugar that is put into wooden molds to cool. This gives the dark sweet an interesting pattern.

Walnut cheese mold, impressed cat design with removable plugs for drainage, 12½″ wide, 19½″ high, **$95.** Iowa.

Tin chocolate molds, left to right: Santa by chimney, 3½″ wide, 5½″high, **$45.** Santa, 2½″ wide, 4½″ high; **$39.** Small Santa, 2″ wide, 3½″ high, **$35.** Santa on donkey, 4¼″ wide, 5½″ high, **$60.** Iowa.

Tin lamb chocolate mold, made in France, 9″ wide, 3″ deep, 6¼″ high, **$65.** Illinois.

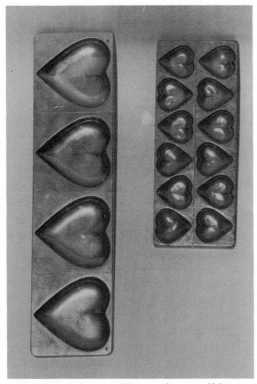

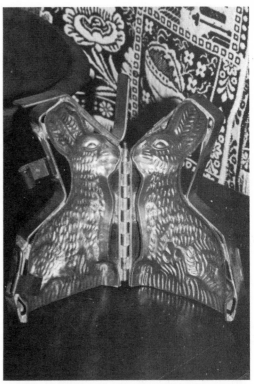

Heart chocolate molds: twelve small hearts mold, 8″ long, 3¼″ wide, **$52.** Mold with four large hearts, 12¼″ long, 3¼″ wide, **$52.** Iowa.

Rabbit chocolate mold, 5″ wide, 8½″ high, **$55.** Indiana.

Copper animal chocolate mold, **$125.** Iowa.

Tin Santa chocolate mold, 10½″×13½″, **$48.** Iowa.

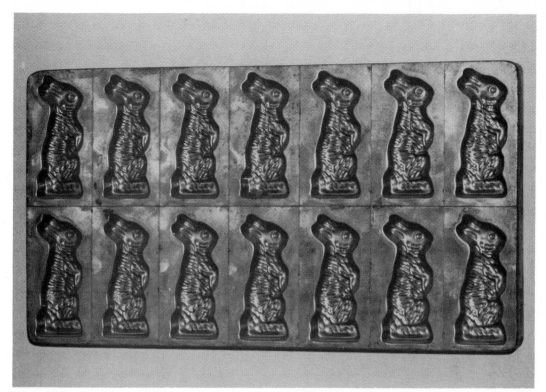

Tin rabbit chocolate mold, 13¼″ long, 7″ wide, **$39.** Iowa.

Tin chocolate molds: turkey, 3¾″ wide, 4½″ high, **$15.** Boy with rabbits, 5½″ wide, 4½″ high, **$32.** Indian, 2¾″ wide, 5½″ high, **$35.** Illinois.

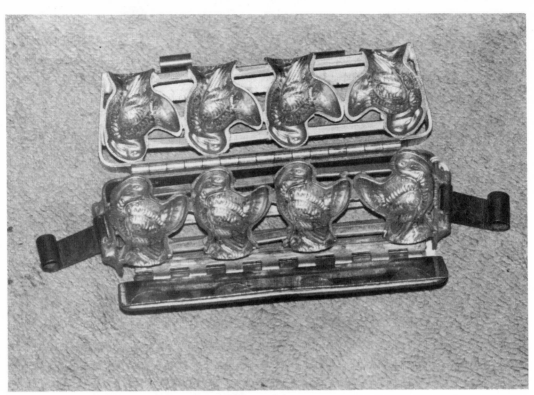

Tin turkey chocolate mold, 8″ long, **$30.** Alabama.

Maple sugar molds: single heart, 4″ wide, 8″ long, 2″ deep, **$80.** Six hearts, 4″ wide, 13″ long, **$90.** Iowa.

Pewter is the norm for ice cream molds. They are heavy in appearance compared to the candy forms. Patriotic themes such as shields, flags, or George Washington on a hatchet head are appreciated, and bring a slightly higher price than the more mundane bells or turkeys. A great variety of subjects is available. Ice cream (formerly called cream ice, frozen milk, or ice milk) was enjoyed by Europeans in the 1500s. It was served at George Washington's Mount Vernon in the late 1700s, and by the mid-1800s it was produced commercially.

Bakers, too, had help in the let's-make-it-pretty area. Pies are an all-American treat, perhaps because wild berries and fruits abounded, and were available for the picking. Crimpers (also called pie trimmers or sealers) were used and had several duties since they cut cookies or pastry, outlined pie edges, and sealed the two crusts together. Rare examples may

Maple sugar mold, New England origin, signed "D. F.," 7¾″ long, 3½″ wide, 1½″ deep, **$250.** Indiana.

Four-part maple sugar house mold that fits into a square; each part 3″ wide, 6¼″ high, **$150.** Ohio.

Pewter ice cream molds from left to right: shield, S. & Co., 4″×3½″, **$62.** Santa Claus, S. & Co., 4½″ high, **$62.** Candle not marked, 3½″ diameter, 5″ high, **$58.** Flag, E. & Co., N.Y., 4″ wide, 2¼″ high, **$62.** Iowa.

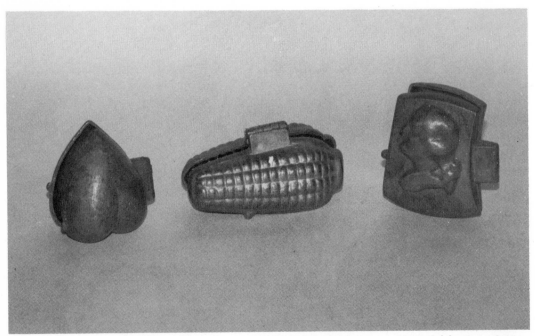

Pewter ice cream molds from left to right: heart not marked, 3½″×3¼″, **$44.** Ear of corn, not marked, 5″ long, 2½″ high, **$46.** George Washington, E. & Co., N.Y., 3½″ wide, 4″ high, **$52.** Iowa.

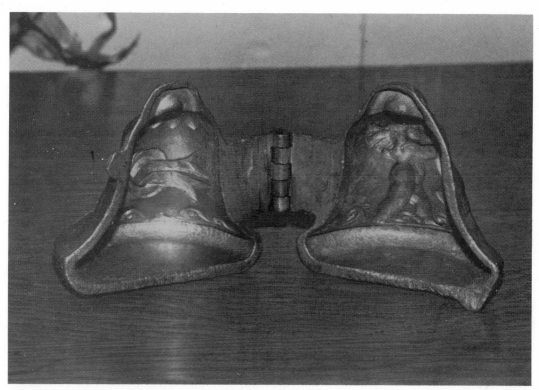

Pewter ice cream mold, bell shaped, **$45.** Iowa.

Pewter ice cream molds from left to right: cupid in a heart, 3″×4″, **$46.50.** Turkey, 4″×4″, **$46.50.** Airplane, E. & Co., 5″×4½″, **$49.50.** Iowa.

Crimpers from left to right: brass and wood, **$35.** 1856 penny and wood, **$125.** Brass and wood, **$45.** Tiger maple and brass, **$70.** Pewter, **$125.** Scrimshaw, **$350.** Delft **$85.** All brass, **$45.** All wood, **$95.** All wood, **$25.** Indiana.

Springerle rolling pin for cookies with fifteen hand-carved designs; elephant, horn, clown, etc., 14″ long, **$575.** Indiana.

include points for pricking bottom crusts or making vents in top crusts. Old crimpers may be made entirely of brass or the wheels may be of brass with wooden handles. Scrimshaw examples (carvings on whalebone) created by sailors on their long, lonely whale hunting voyages of the 1830–1880 period are expensive and difficult to acquire. Wood, iron, and those with porcelain wheels were also old. Tin-plated and aluminum crimpers are usually from the early 1900s. A collection was photographed in the basement kitchen of a pre-1819 home, and among the unusual models was an 1856 one-cent piece converted into a crimper. Tiger maple with the stripes that give it its name is not a common wood, but a handle made from it can be seen in the photograph. Tinglazed, blue-and-white delft earthenware from Delft, Holland or from England forms a wheel. Crimpers are varied in details.

Cookies made with a springerle rolling pin must have been fun to eat. Each had designs of animals, people, birds, boats, stars, hearts, or whatever subjects interested the wood carver who made the board or carved the rolling pin that formed the thin cookies with their neat panels. One rolling pin sighted was incomplete. The man who started to carve it finished several rows, and that was it. The prints were pressed into the dough after it was in the pan, and were cut apart. A crimper could perform this task.

Yellow cornbread sticks shaped to resemble an ear of corn are appropriate. It is best to preheat the pan before inserting the batter. The sticks are more apt to come out easily. Molds of this type are being made currently.

Buttermaking was a profitable farm industry in the last half of the 1800s, and it was customary to package it in pounds, or half pounds. It was possi-

Hand-carved springerle cookie mold, 6¾″ × 7″, **$600.** Indiana.

Miniature cornbread mold, 4″ wide, 8½″ long, **$55.** Kansas.

Springerle pewter cookie mold mounted on wooden back with metal handle, 7½″ wide, 4″ deep, 1¼″ high, **$375.** Indiana.

Butter molds from left to right: one-pound leaf design, 4″ wide, 7″ long, **$56.** Eight designs on two-pound mold with quarter-pound divisions, 5¼″ wide, 11¼″ long, **$139.50.** One-pound mold with four designs, 6″ wide, 5¼″ long, **$69.50.** Iowa.

Swan butter mold, **$110.** Virginia.

ble, however, to purchase other sizes including two pounders. When these pats were packed into molds that had patterns cut into their surfaces, the butter acquired a raised design. Early molds were carved by hand, but by the late 1850s most were commercially produced, although they generally retained hand-cut touches.

Molds have been around for centuries. In the 1600s, Europeans liked to use them, and immigrants in the 1700s brought butter molds to this country. There are various types available. Some are in a two-part box formation, and the butter is extracted by pushing the print to one end to slide the base up and out. Customarily, there were decorated sections so that the butter could be cut apart into smaller serving sizes, convenient one-fourth pounds, for example.

A plunger type consisted of three parts — a bowl or cup, a movable, removable handle (stick), and the carved plate. The parts could be separated into three units by unscrewing the handle that had wooden threads. This made the mold easy to clean. A tamp (a flat-headed masher) packed the butter in the mold, forcing it into the cutout design. When the butter was set, it was pushed out by the plunger.

A stamp is one piece, and consists of a handle with a print attachment that was pressed into the butter. Besides being attractive, the designs that were created identified the farm from which the butter came. If the product were choice, customers looked for that particular decoration.

Molds were moistened before use and can be expected to retain stains with perhaps a slight suggestion of a buttery odor. A mellow, smooth look develops

Butter mold, print and tamp, **$125.** Iowa.

with age and handling or a crack might show. This alerts a buyer, "This is old, not a reproduction" (repro for short). Molds made of glass were not too practical as they could chip, crack, or break easily. They are being made currently.

Candle molds are discussed in Chapter 4, which tells about lighting devices. Making candles was a farmwife's chore, usually the final step in saving everything possible after beef cattle were slaughtered in the fall in order to augment the winter's food supply and provide leather for shoes and boots. The beef tallow was melted and enough candles were made to last the family for a year. Molds were not set out as interesting decorative objects or conversation pieces. They performed useful functions in American homes of the past.

Butter stamps from left to right: round AA Bradford, 4″ diameter, **$150.** Round Blawdty, 5″ diameter, **$225.** Round acorn, 3½″ diameter, **$110.** Iowa.

Butter stamps from left to right: oval Ruth Cox, 7″ long, **$350.** Round Margarett Pringle, 4″ diameter, **$185.** Half-round floral and leaves, 7″ long, **$185.** Iowa.

Acorn butter mold, 5¾″ diameter, **$60.** Pennsylvania.

Glass butter mold with cow and Florentine print, **$125.** Glass butter mold with cow print, **$150.** Ohio.

Butter prints from left to right: eagle, 5¼″ diameter, **$400.** Cow, 4½″ diameter, **$185.** Two birds and foliage, 4¾″ diameter, **$225.** Indiana.

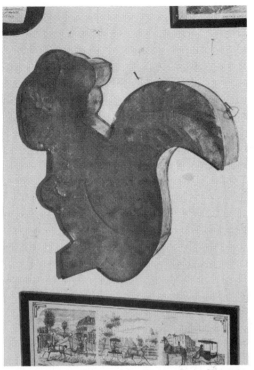

Eagle butter mold, 4¼″ diameter, **$325.**
Illinois.

Tin squirrel cake mold, 13″ wide, 14″ high,
$65. Iowa.

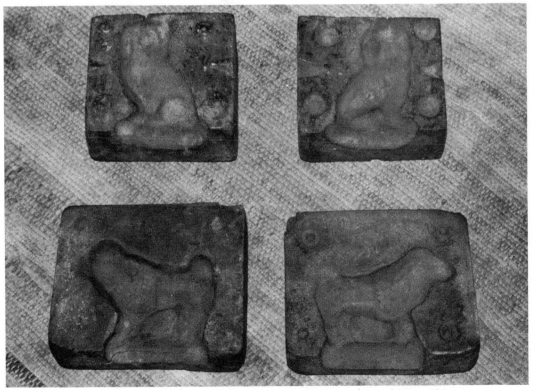

Redware dog molds; top 4¾″ × 4¼″, **$28.** Bottom 5¾″ × 4¾″, **$28.** Ohio.

Three-tube candle mold, 4″ wide, 7″ high, **$44.** Iowa.

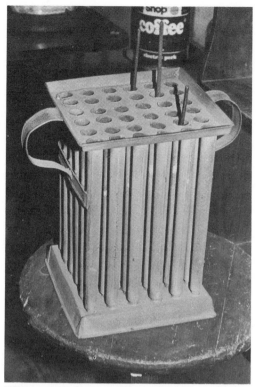

Thirty-six-tube candle mold, 8″ wide, 8″ deep, 10½″ high, **$175.** Connecticut.

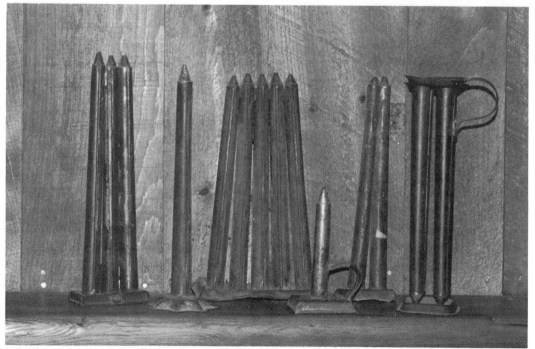

Candle molds from left to right: three-tube mold, **$52.** One-tube mold, **$42.** Five-tube mold, **$65.** Small one-tube mold, **$42.** Two-tube mold, **$46.** Four-tube mold, **$48.** Taller molds are 11″ high, and small mold is 5½″ high. Iowa.

Single candle mold, 11″ high, **$65.** Iowa.

Eight-tube candle mold, 6″ wide, 3½″ deep, 10½″ high, **$110.** Indiana.

10 Artwork from the needle and loom

A woman exclaimed, "Oh, what a shame!" as she and her friend examined articles to be offered at auction. "Someone ripped this pretty bedspread in two." A knowledgeable young woman enjoyed this remark, and when she bid eighteen dollars, people wondered why. She knew it was a coverlid (the archaic term for coverlet) that was hand-woven on a four-harness loom in two pieces that were meant to be sewn together to form a full counterpane (bed covering). Because she knew, this antiques devotee carried away a treasure worth several hundred dollars.

Overshot coverlet, woven in two pieces and seamed together, blue and white, **$300.** Iowa.

In the United States, most homes had their own textile making units that called for family cooperation and participation. Linen, made from flax, is a strong cloth. Its tough, home-grown stalks had to be soaked to rot off and expose the fibers enclosed between the bark and the core, then pounded, scraped, and combed by manpower until the women could take over the work. Wool was sheared from the sheep by the men. Then, the women washed out the grease, grass, and dirt; sorted it, cleaned out the burs, and carded (combed) it. Cotton, likewise, had to be grown, cared for, and processed before it could be spun.

It was better to dye the wool, flax, or cotton in its raw state, but coloring could be added to skeins of yarn or to the woven cloth. The second method was the least satisfactory. The two most common dye sources were the roots of the madder plant for red and the indigo plant for blue. The fields and forests offered many other dye materials to dig or pick. Yellow might come from the bark of walnut or hickory trees or the leaves of a peach tree. Black came from alder, and butternut yielded brown. Enough dye had to be boiled at one time to complete a project because a second batch would differ from the first. Plants picked a few weeks apart also produced a slightly different tone. The soft, warm, earthen hues that resulted from long simmering with a mixture of ingredients in the large open kettles were worth the trouble. They have lasted for many generations to be appreciated when coverlets made of homespun yarn are viewed.

A long time ago, the man of the family might have made a loom for his wife out of hand-hewn beams. She strung lengthwise threads called warp close together in regular parallel rows on this frame, and then laced in crosswise threads (weft or woof) by using a shuttle that was somewhat like a large needle.

The weaver raised and lowered the lengthwise lines by hand to permit the shuttle to go back and forth as she alternated the rows from over-under to under-over, leaving behind a trail of horizontal yarn intertwined with the base threads to create a simple weave. After each crossing, the horizontals would be pressed down close to each other. Different patterns were achieved by changing the way the threads were interlaced.

Later, a device called the harness operated with a foot pedal was installed to raise and lower the lengthwise threads automatically. When a movable frame called a batten was added, it pressed the crosswise threads tightly into place. A busy loom was noisy with its clackety-clacks, thuds, and thump, thumps. Much as a singer watches notes on sheet music, the weaver studied a piece of paper with lines and numbers, her pattern that guided her hands as she created a coverlet.

Each spread received a picturesque name. ''Rose in the Wilderness,'' ''Wonder of the Forest,'' ''Sunrise on the Walls of Troy,'' ''Islands of the Sea,'' ''Granny's Garden,'' or ''Winding Leaves

Wooden tape loom often given as personal gift to wives or sweethearts; used to make personal articles such as braids, belts, suspenders, 10¼" wide, 29" long, **$295.** Iowa.

Coverlet, red and blue, **$295.** South Carolina.

197

and Folding Windows" are romantic titles. Occasionally, the same or a similar pattern acquired a different name in other sections of the country. For example, in Kentucky there was a "Missouri Trouble," which in North Carolina was designated "Spectacles" and elsewhere was "Mountain Flowers." Political and historical events inspired "Indian Warfare," "Whig Rose," "Washington's Victory," or "Lee's Surrender."

The first homespun coverlets in this country probably warmed the shivering immigrants as they crossed the Atlantic Ocean. Perhaps some were on the Pilgrim's ship, the *Mayflower,* as it sailed into Plymouth Harbor in 1620. These spreads were a touch of home brought to a new land.

Many of the earliest coverlets were woven by women in their homes and by professional weavers. There are sources that mention itinerant laborers who set up looms in a locale and moved on when business began to slow down. In some sections of the country, slaves were trained in weaving skills.

Coverlets are classified by their characteristics, and four main types emerge.

Overshot coverlet on blanket rack, **$465.** Illinois.

The Overshot. When skips were made with the wool overshooting the threads in the loom, they would rest on top of the foundation. A flatter, more tightly woven pattern was created when there were no long skips. By looking at and feeling these almost bumplike top lines that are slightly elevated above the surface, it is possible to determine that the coverlet is an overshot. Geometric patterns were prominent in this skip-stitch form.

The Double Weave. Two warps (lengthwise) and two woof threads (horizontal) are created simultaneously, one above the other. They are united as one at the pattern points, but can be pulled apart elsewhere by gently separating them with the hand, almost as fingers explore pockets. Geometric patterns predominated.

The Summer and Winter. The weaving on the front of a summer-winter coverlet is reversed on the back. A dark pattern against a light base shows on one side. Turn the coverlet over, and the opposite is true. The design will be

Winter-summer weave jacquard coverlet, red and natural; dark background on left is the winter while the light background on the right is the summer; note the misspelling "manufacterd," **$285.** Tennessee.

Hooked rug, in red, pinks, and grays, 26″×34½″, **$225.** Iowa.

white on a dark backing. These spreads, more tightly woven than the overshots, are thought to have originated in America, perhaps in Pennsylvania. They are light in weight so that they provide a covering suitable for all seasons. Sides could be switched to expose either the colored or light background to fit the feel of that time of year. Geometric designs prevailed.

The Jacquard. With the invention of the Jacquard loom, a hand-operated machine began to take over the production of coverlets. Seamless ones with complex patterns and complicated borders came into being. A weaver could throw his shuttle an average of forty inches which limited the width of his product. The new loom had a flying shuttle. No longer was it necessary to sew two or three woven pieces together to complete one bed cover, unless a Jacquard attachment was placed on an older small-sized loom. Many times, the corners were designed to include the maker's name, the county, state, and the date. Perhaps, the owner's name was added. This has helped greatly in tracing the development of the industry. Boston Town, with sailing vessels in the harbor and a row of buildings including churches, was one favored border. When oriental pagodas were interspersed, the outline frequently was referred to as Christian and Heathen. Fruits, flowers, animals, or birds set off the elaborate designs of the coverlets. Patriotic symbols such as the eagle and busts of the presidents were popular. Even though the patterns were fancy, a professional could finish a coverlet in a day instead of taking weeks to complete a project.

A brief history will help to show why this invention was important. The nineteenth century had barely toddled in when the Jacquard loom, developed by Joseph Marie Jacquard (1752–1834) of France was exhibited in 1801. Like a player piano, it had a belt of cards punched with holes arranged to produce the designs in the weave. This activated the harnesses, devices that raised and lowered the lengthwise threads automatically. The older looms had four harnesses. Now, there could be ten times that many. The weavers could buy standard cards or punch their own to create figured patterns.

French weavers opposed this invention because they felt it would destroy their skilled trade, and a mob seized and broke up a loom. Jacquard himself hustled to escape alive. His invention prevailed, however, and was adopted by professionals. It was a couple of decades later, about 1820, before it reached the United States coastal areas. Slowly, it migrated westward, reaching Indiana in the late 1830s. For a time, hand and machine weaving co-existed, but when professionals advertised that they would accept the homespun, home-dyed yarns and make coverlets from them at discount prices, their offers were hard to resist. Besides, the plainer geometric patterns no longer were in style. Instead, the Jacquard loom's large, bright flowers, stars, birds, and the like were preferred. Gradually, the women deserted their spinning wheels and their dye pots as factory yarns and colors took over. In general, by 1870, the interest in coverlets had waned.

Frugal — that word describes housewives who utilized any good material clipped from old clothing that no longer could be refashioned into hand-me-downs for someone smaller to wear. From the hoof (sheep) or plant (cotton and flax) to the loom, cloth required hours of labor to make. Every scrap was cherished.

Someone decided rugs could be created from scraps. A magazine from the 1830s recommended that children

Hooked rug depicting maple sugaring time, in black, reds, and brown, 19″×35″, **$250.** Iowa.

Hooked rug depicting bear emerging from woods and stealing loaf of bread, 18″×37½″, **$225.** Iowa.

should braid mats, but hooked rugs possibly date from the late 1700s. Homespun wool, unbleached cotton or linen, preferably loose woven, formed the foundation for early examples. Later, burlap backing was used. Yarns or rags of various colors cut into narrow strips were needed. A pattern was sketched on the foundation, and a pencil-sized piece of wood or metal with a hook at the end pulled the loops up through to the top of the cloth. The loops were inserted as close together as possible. When the pattern was completed, a plain border could outline the design. The excess edges were turned under and sewed down.

The production peak was reached in the mid-1800s, but faded away as the century closed. New Englanders were creative crafters of hooked rugs. However, women in rural areas elsewhere likewise enjoyed making them. It was a useful way to recycle rags or scraps, and economical as well.

Subject matter, not age per se, attracts interest. All show signs of wear, but condition, the workmanship, and the harmony of the colors should receive consideration. The story of maple sugar gathering on the farm is depicted on one rug. The sap house where the water is boiled off until the syrup remains, the men carrying buckets, and the ox waiting to pull his load are all in the maple grove.

Another shows a woman in a long, full skirt baking bread in an outdoor beehive oven. In the original form of the story from Granville, Massachusetts, she set the fresh loaves on a rock. While her back was turned, a bear ambled out of the woods and walked off munching on her bread. A table replaces the rock in the picture. Any animals have appeal.

Samplers are another textile which have an interesting derivation. Originally, adults took a strip of cloth of the desired shape or size and carefully filled it with embroidery or lace patterns they wished to remember and preserve. Thus, early samplers were remembrances of the past in needlework. Sometime during the 1500s, it became the fashion for young girls to make samplers as they learned to sew. It was also a way for the skillful to show their ability, no matter what their ages. English wills dating from the sixteenth century mention this type of needle art as do various literary works.

Hooked rug showing horse's head within horseshoe, brownish red, green, and brown, **$225.** Iowa.

Hooked rug, two black dogs with pink and gray border, 21″×38″. **$250.** Iowa.

American sampler on homespun signed "Mary Ann Thorson," 26″×19¾″. **$690.** Georgia.

An 1852 floral and alphabet sampler by Mary Jane Starr of the Starr Piano Co., Richmond, Indiana, 17½" × 21½". **$550.** Indiana.

English sampler; notice the crowns and foo dogs that are found on many English samplers, **$450.** Ohio.

Aurora, Indiana boarding school sampler, 14" × 15", **$375.** Indiana.

English sampler; notice crowns by Amens near top, made by Susan Spicer in 1804, 17¼" × 21½", **$925.** Georgia.

The name of the needleworker, her age, and the date were frequently included in the pattern. Occasionally, a sampler looks as if the threads that tell the age have been pulled out. Perhaps, a vain woman disliked having people know how old she was.

Back in the early 1800s, every female child had to be able to sew a variety of stitches, and four was the customary age to start. A wee youngster's hands were trained to do intricate work even though she dreaded sitting still and she might prick her fingers on the troublesome, slippery needle.

Samplers seemed to change gradually from the long, narrow, simple, cross-stitched type of the colonial period to the more intricate ones of the early 1800s with their pictures of animals, people, scenes, and angels. Square shapes slowly replaced the vertical frames until, as the art was fading out at the century's end, horizontal samplers were acceptable. Female seminaries, which were boarding schools for girls, taught sewing as well as the usual academic subjects. An occasional piece of needlework will mention a particular school; thus, in many ways, samplers help preserve a record of the past. If small crowns are present, the work was probably completed in England.

The sorrowful mourning pictures are of English derivation. Outlines were stamped on a paper background, and the design was embroidered with floss. Some details could be painted in, such as the flesh tones on the hands, feet, and face of the sad one. Many of these were imported as stamped to be worked by young ladies enrolled in the seminaries. Victorians seemed to like themes that served as a memorial. These pictures were in fashion throughout the nineteenth century. Since they were introduced at the beginning of the 1800s, their reign was longer than that of

Queen Victoria, who ruled in England from 1837 to 1901.

English women and schoolgirls also adopted Berlin work (at times called worsted work), which German matrons made as early as the 1780s. About the time that century ended, printed designs on charts similar to graph paper became available, so that women could count corresponding holes in needlework canvas and execute the design in worsted wool. They made covers for piano seats, footstools, sofas, chairs, or other objects. About 1860, a machine was invented that punched perforations on cardboard. Women could use thread and yarn to fill in printed designs to make a picture. This "tapestry needlework" featured favorite sayings such as "Remember Me," "He Cares for You," "Home Sweet Home," and "Be True in Heart." While this artform was widespread in England from about the 1830s through the 1880s, it peaked in the United States around 1840. Large stitches and thick, brightly colored wool highlighted these sentimental expressions.

Mourning picture, 20½″ × 20¾″, **$2,900.** Iowa.

Mourning picture, 13¾″ × 16″, **$2,100.** Iowa.

What's Home Without a Mother, Berlin work done on punched paper background, 24½″ × 28½″, **$110.** Iowa.

Home Sweet Home, Berlin work done on punched paper background, 22½″ × 18½″, **$98.** Iowa.

Theorem or velvet painting by Bathia E. Stang in 1820, N.Y., 20½″×19½″, **$300.** Iowa.

Theorem or velvet painting by Bathia E. Stang in 1820, N.Y., 20½″×19½″, **$300.** Iowa.

A different effect resulted when stencils called theorems were used to paint designs on cloth. Velvet was the usual selection, but rich satin, silk, or even common muslin could serve for backgrounds. A theorem was secured on top of the fabric, and paint was applied to the open space. Additional theorems, layered one at a time over the first, could create a more complicated design. Pupils enrolled in the female seminaries established by the strict Moravian religious sect scorned stencils and executed freehand drawings on velvet. When stencils were used on furniture, the design was cut in oiled or greased paper and placed over the article before the paint was applied. Theorems could be effective on paper as well.

This chapter has dealt with cloth-related art objects, so why should a tin cow receive mention? Sometimes, designs are cut out and sewed onto a quilt patch. The resulting cover is called an appliquéd quilt. For example, the outline of a cow was traced on a piece of cloth, and cut out to become one of the appliquéd blocks. It is a template or pattern. Many types are being reproduced today. A quilt top is commonly assembled from pieces of cloth cut out and precisely sewn together to form a design. There is a filling and a bottom layer. These are stitched together in lines or patterns. Knowledgeable people expect quilts to have thirteen tiny stitches to the inch and not more than three inches between the quilting lines. Seven-year-old girls, with perhaps three or four years of stitching behind them, were trained to complete their first quilt and continue making them until they had a baker's dozen to take with them as part of their dowry when they married, usually in their teens. Each piece had to be fitted exactly right or the whole pattern could go awry. Log Cabin, Star of Bethlehem, Wild Goose Chase, Sawtooth, Virginia Lily, and Pin-

Tin template for cutting designs for a quilt patch, 10″ wide, 8½″ high, **$150.** Ohio.

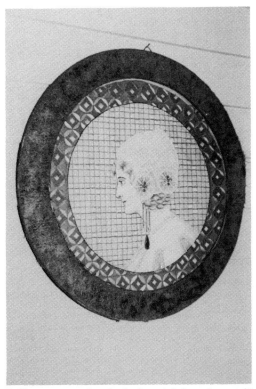

Folk art portrait of a lady with lace hat and lace outline on collar, 22" diameter, **$85.** Iowa.

A family heading westward to relocate might receive a quilt with the names of neighbors embroidered on it as a remembrance to carry across the miles to a new home. Quilts were a part of the social life when the United States was growing up. They were made from the colonial period on as a necessary way to save every piece of cloth and to provide warm bed covers. The art has experienced a revival in recent years.

Featured in the Color Section are several examples that show colors and varied designs of the quilts fashioned by homemakers or young ladies in days gone by.

wheel were some of the fanciful names these coverings acquired.

A quilting party was a social event where women met to sew the three layers of a quilt together. It was held tightly in a frame around which the friends sat. A woman tells a story about her great aunt whom everyone liked. The aunt's stitches were not up to standard, but no one wanted to offend her. After she left, the hostess would remove her work and redo it. No one ever told her about her inadequacies as a quilter.

Friendship quilts, pieces supplied by friends or relatives, were presented to brides-to-be. It was bad luck to have hearts in the design unless a maiden was "spoken for" (engaged). Friends designed their own blocks for the wedding quilts and sprinkled them liberally with hearts.

11 Folk art gems

When an untutored man picks up a knife and sits whittling, he is creating folk art. Some is skillfully executed and some is not. But, interest is being focused on carved objects from America's past.

Back in 1925, the Paris Exposition Internationale des Arts Decoratifs et Industriels Modernes featured luxurious fabrics, delicate glass, leather, silver, and wooden objects. Hand workmanship was stressed. Geometric forms were emphasized. In an attempt to go modern, designers sought zigzag lines, angles, and cubes to escape from the flowing, sensuous curves, florid decorations, and natural motifs of the art nouveau (late 1800s, early 1900s) period. Garish colors frequently were used. The name of this artistic style was an abbreviated one inspired by the Paris Exposition. It was termed art deco (late 1920s – 1930s), and the common interpretation was not exactly the elegance that the originators had anticipated.

Art Deco period bell boy, red jacket, white pants, black boots, 34″ high, **$325.** Iowa.

Another fair provided dated items of historical significance that are attractive to collectors. When the one-hundredth birthday of the United States was celebrated at the Centennial Exposition of 1876 in Philadelphia, souvenirs were available to the thousands who attended. On one item, a Moslem shrine is hand carved on olive wood. It is the Dome of the Rock (Mosque of Omar) that was built on the site of the ancient Temple of Jerusalem, destroyed by the Romans in the year 70 A.D.

Currently there is a trend toward the appreciation of crafts created by Americans of African ancestry, or of articles that depict people with this background. During the Civil War, some of the slaves fought to help secure their freedom, and a uniformed, dancing soldier is shown here.

The life of the native Americans, the Indians, can receive emphasis through carvings. Their handcrafted jewelry, baskets, and rugs are sought eagerly.

Other examples of wood carvings follow. The first one is of interest because it was made in Pennsylvania by a prisoner of World War II (1941–1945). On his back, the little figure carries tools of a peaceful trade, a saw and a hatchet, but the man has no arms. Perhaps the war ended before the prisoner completed his task.

It is interesting to compare a Pennsylvania wooden coach with a European look carved about 1840–1860 with one that could be from America's Western heritage. Passengers who climbed up to fill the outside seats on the latter were exposed to the dust of the roads and the elements. When the coach jolted and swayed, it was difficult to maintain one's seat, and the riders would have to hang on tightly. There was an advantage. Passengers paid less for these outside seats.

Woodcarving of woodsman, arms missing, by World War II prisoner, 9″ high, **$65.** Pennsylvania.

Hand-carved olive wood souvenirs from Philadelphia Centennial Exposition of 1876; left is 3″ diameter, **$20.** Right is 4¾″ diameter, **$35.** Connecticut.

Have you ever heard of a Sunday toy? The Sabbath was strictly observed as a day of rest and respectful worship. Only necessary chores such as feeding and milking the cows were done. In some denominations, children were not permitted to play on that day. They could read the Bible or books that dealt with church-related themes. There were games such as Bible Authors or a quiz called Scripture Cards that were acceptable because they were Bible oriented. A Noah's Ark from the late 1800s could slide under the line because it helped children re-enact that Old Testament story.

Walking or dancing wooden toy with red coat, yellow legs, black tie and trim, 5″ wide, 13½″ high, **$45.** Iowa.

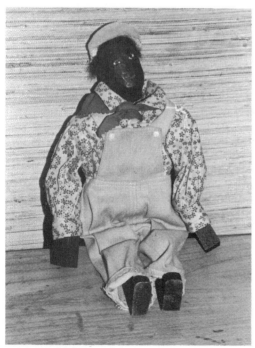

Wooden doll with blue bib overalls, 15″ high, **$80.** Iowa.

Sheet metal sprinkler made in Defiance, Ohio, 30″ high, **$195.** Georgia.

Wooden Indian beating drum, 7″ high, **$70.** Iowa.

Wooden Indian in canoe, 14″ long, 8½″ high, **$195.** Connecticut.

Wooden Indian chief and maiden; brown, red, white, and black, 7½" high, **$225.** Iowa.

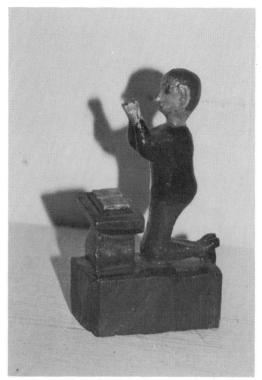

Woodcarving of man in prayer, early 1900s, 4½" high, **$65.** Iowa.

Dancing soldier, circa 1861, 8" high, **$195.** Connecticut.

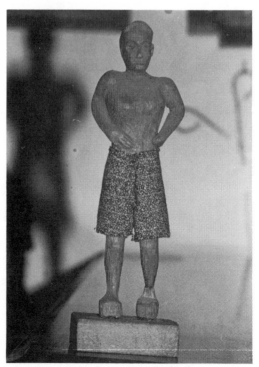

Woodcarving of man in cloth shorts, circa 1940, 8" high, **$65.** Iowa.

Wooden passenger pigeon decoy, purple, red, gray, and black, 12″ high, **$135.** Iowa.

Perching owl done by Theodore A. Bishop in Litchfield County, Connecticut, 4″ wide, 24″ high, **$150.** Iowa.

Two roosters and a giraffe carved by Stanley Walicki, circa 1950, 8″ and 10″ high, **$70.** Pennsylvania.

Possum with babies in pouch, 12″ long, 12″ high, **$265.** Michigan.

Gesso (plaster of paris) camel, 7″ long, 7″ high, **$165.** Connecticut.

St. Bernard, circa 1940, New Hampshire, 3½″ high, **$55.** Pennsylvania.

Hand-carved bloodhound, World War II vintage, 4½″ long, 4¼″ high, **$60.** Pennsylvania.

Cat, 2″ high; pig, 2¼″ long, **$35** each. Pennsylvania.

Swiss ram with glass eyes, 5¼″ long, 4″ high, **$50.** Pennsylvania.

Horse on platform, 13″ long, 12″ high, **$195.** Connecticut.

Old World stage, Pennsylvania woodcarving, circa 1840, 12″ long, 5½″ high, **$425.** Georgia.

Road coach, 10½″ long, 5½″ wide, 9″ high, **$145.** Pennsylvania.

Carved ball in cage, 6¼ " high, **$45.** Illinois.

City hall model, 16″ wide, 10½ ″ deep, 17″ high, **$85.** Iowa.

Colorful, hollow wooden blocks with their lithographed paper coverings were made in graduated sizes. These could be inserted, one inside the other, until the largest box held them all. Such nested sets were popular in the late 1800s. Their pictures were child-oriented, and the addition of the letters of the alphabet hopefully prompted learning skills. In order to make the lithographed design for these blocks, the picture was drawn on a flat, porous stone plate with a greased crayon. Since water and oil don't mix, water was put on and was absorbed where there was no grease. When oiled printing ink was rolled on, it adhered only to the crayon marks. Paper was pressed against the stone to create the prints. Before about 1866, each design was hand-colored. Artists who did this work usually were women. Seated in groups at tables, each filled in a specific hue as the pictures were passed along. When a technique was developed whereby a different printing plate was used for each color, the hand touches were no longer necessary.

There is something jaunty about a weather vane sitting on a barn, garage, or house rooftop. One of the oldest weather instruments, it turns easily on an upright rod to point in the direction from which the wind originates. Since a cock frequently perches there, they are called weathercocks also. A grasshopper found on English buildings immigrated to the New World, and Shem Drowne from Massachusetts created a facsimile to top Faneuil Hall, the building where patriots in Boston assembled in the days prior to the Revolutionary War. Drowne also designed a tall copper Indian with a bow and arrow for the governor's residence. Farm animals represented agricultural interests while seamen selected fish, ships, or mermaids to adorn their wind vanes. They could be made of wood, flat at first, then carved and raised a bit. Iron, copper, brass, and zinc, or combinations

Water mill with two moving male figures, early twentieth century, 25″ wide, 14″ deep, 15″ high, **$550.** Iowa.

Close-up of man pushing cart, 5″ high.

Electrically animated cobbler who turns head and pounds; cardboard background, **$625.** Iowa.

Noah's ark and animals, 6″ long, 4″ high, **$145.** Connecticut.

Horse pulltoy with leather harness, 9″ long, 8″ high, **$230.** Iowa.

Pyramid and ABC blocks of diminishing size that nest together; pictures on blocks are lithographs over wood; sizes graduate from 2″ wide to 7¼″ wide, **$375.** Indiana.

Rooster weather vane, 24″ wide, 19″ high, **$895.** Connecticut.

Log constructed and carved rocking horse with leather seat, 34″ long, 14″ wide, 28″ high, **$600.** Ohio.

Man playing piano, circa 1920, 7½" wide, 10" deep, 10¼" high, **$275.** Illinois.

Building carved in wood, nineteenth century, 14" diameter, 19" high, **$145.** Connecticut.

of metals, were used to form the rods and figures. It is not unusual to find holes in the designs at which farm lads aimed their rifles in target practice.

Another farm animal was the Fairbury bull. This name refers to the town in Nebraska where a windmill weight shaped as a bull was cast in iron. The mill's wheel of blades is held with its face toward the wind by a rudder. The gusts of wind strike the blades, forcing them to revolve and produce power to pump water out of wells. Similar weights were made in other locales. Thus, an Elgin rooster doesn't crow, but its folksy outline represents Illinois' contribution to this art. Since they were farm aids in the Midwest in the late 1800s, the East both lacks and likes them, and higher prices can be anticipated there than in the Great Plains area.

When a man carried his long musket, he slung a powder horn on a cord over his shoulder and carried a small pouch with a bullet mold, bullets, and wadded flax pad for swabbing the gun barrel. Usually, the hollow horn once adorned the head of an ox or cow. Caps of wood were placed at each end of the horn to contain the powder. When the musket required loading, the cap on the small end was removed, and the powder was poured into the muzzle. After the trigger on a flintlock weapon was pulled, the flint struck a piece of steel that set off the powder charge and fired the bullet. Flintlocks were used from the 1600s until around 1850. Some horns were decorated. If a Tennessee hill man incised a reclining, scantily covered lady on his polished powder horn, his companions probably appreciated his artwork.

What's a wooden or scrimshaw busk? Busks were stays kept in place by slipping each one into its own individual elongated pocket stitched on the under-

Rooster weather vane; rooster 13½″ high; arrow 22″ long, **$195.** Indiana.

Rooster weather vane swivels on stand; made of gray metal with a red comb and a hole for the eye, 12″ wide, 12″ high, **$275.** Iowa.

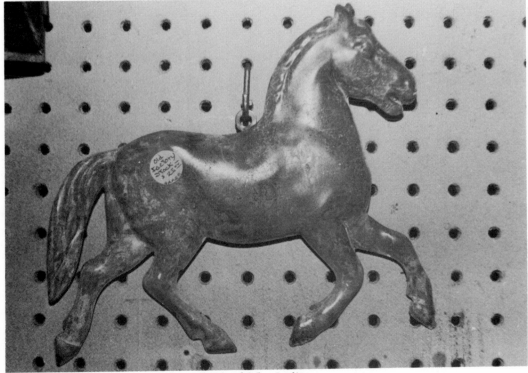

Factory stock horse, 9″ wide, 8″ high, **$25.** Indiana.

Nineteenth-century weather vane with tin bird, iron arrow, and wooden base support, 41″ long, 36″ high, **$175.** Connecticut.

Horse weather vane, **$175.** Indiana.

Cow weather vane with four observable bullet holes, 23″ long, 8½″ high, **$245.** Wisconsin.

Remains of car-and-driver weather vane with bullet holes in car, 12″ long, 7½″ high, **$57.50.** Iowa.

Arrow weather vane, 29″ long, **$245.** Iowa.

Fairbury bull, a windmill weight, cast by the Fairbury Windmill Company of Fairbury, Nebraska, late nineteenth century, 24″ long, **$385.** Iowa.

Powder horn with carving, circa 1870, 20″ long, **$350.** Indiana.

side of a dress. These stiff slats sought to control tummy curves that wanted to bulge. The wooden one to the left in the picture with its cut design is older than the scrimshaw example that dates to about 1830 because of the hair styles and attire of the ladies depicted on it.

Back in the 1830s to 1880s, New England cities were the centers for a wealthy whaling industry. One product was whale oil that served as fuel for lamps. The sailors who hunted for these huge sea mammals were away from home several years at a time. Taking the raw material they had at hand, whalebone or walrus tusks, they would carve gifts. These are called scrimshaws.

Baleen whales lack teeth. Instead they have horny plates with a bristlelike fringe in their upper jaws that strains their food. Whalebone from the baleen whale, decorated with incised (cut in) hearts, initials, sentimental statements, dates, and other ornamentation, was shaped into spoons, boxes, or stays for women's dresses (busks).

How can a groom-to-be say "I love you" to his prospective wife in a delightful manner? The Pennsylvania Dutch knew a way. Make a bride's box. Tradition says the young lover created an oval box out of thin wood, pegged or nailed together. If he desired, he painted a male and female figure on the lid and included a message of love, inscribed in German. Other swains selected fruits, flowers, or birds for their brightly colored decorations. The young wife slipped her most delicate objects into her bride's box to take to her new home. The custom is thought to have originated in Europe and appeared in America in the late 1700s.

Hand-sawed ash or hickory bentwood bandboxes or those made from lightweight pasteboard were not merely containers for a man's neck bands. They

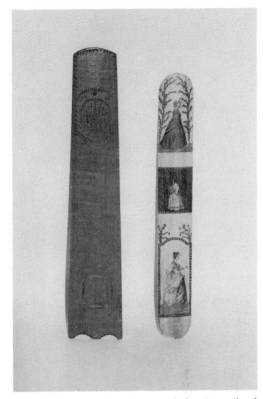

Busks for ladies' garments; left: inscribed design in wood, 14″ long, **$175**. Right: scrimshaw, circa 1830, 13″ long, **$400**. Iowa.

Bride's boxes, 11½″ wide, 19″ deep, 7¾″ high, **$1,200** each. Illinois.

Indian stamped birch bark basket, New England, nineteenth century, lapped construction, 8″ diameter, 7¼″ high, **$85.** Illinois.

Bandbox with New York City Hall on cover, circa 1830, 16″ wide, 13″ high, **$400.** Iowa.

were clutter catchers for storage at home or performed a service similar to present-day, small airplane flight bags. Little articles of apparel, hats, gloves, or other items could be tucked in them for travel. They were used in the late 1700s, but their greatest popularity was about 1820 to 1845. Most of these round or oval containers were covered with wallpaper or paper created for this purpose. Hand-carved wooden blocks could be used to hand stamp designs on the paper that was pasted on the surface. Buildings, current events, figures of people, animals, and flowers were among the motifs. On top of the bandbox in the illustration is the earliest known view of the third New York City Hall, which was completed in 1812.

A man can't carry much in his bare hands. The American Indians knew this, and hundreds of years before discovery of the New World, they wove baskets to assist them as they gathered, hauled, and stored necessities. Archeologists have found fragments to support this fact. Vines, supple willow twigs, reeds, grasses, and splint from oak or ash trees were some of the materials from nature available to weave into carriers. All around the world, people practice such techniques.

Today, women add the country touch to homes with baskets dangling from rafters, or hanging from old porch posts

The same type basket may have many names according to what the owner used it for or in what locale it was found. One form built around a rib outline is called a buttocks basket at times because of its vague resemblance to the human form. Actually, this split construction had a purpose. It distributes the weight so that all the pressure was not placed on the center of the bottom. The division permitted the basket to be a hip hugger, thus helping an individual support the load. Some of the buttocks baskets' names earned from its shape or its make are rib, gizzard, melon, hip, or pack.

A family inherited a "What's this?" item that was given to an aunt by her music pupils as a token of appreciation. It was a triple pedestal box, strange in its outline. Every bit of its surface was chip carved (small notches cut out) on thin layers of wood retrieved from cigar boxes. The one assigned to select the gift for the teacher evidently appreciated folk art or wanted to give a present with a difference to someone whose preferences and tastes were unknown. She selected a tramp art box.

Chip carving, making notches in the edges of wood, did not require expensive tools. A pocketknife would do. An itinerant farmhand sitting and whittling, a convalescent waiting for his strength to return, an out-of-work man wander-ing the countryside looking for bread and board money, a World War I prisoner awaiting release (1917–1918), an old man seeking a pastime — anyone could take out a jacknife and whittle. The work was customarily done on thin cigar boxes that frequently were available for the asking or for a slight charge. Wood from vegetable and fruit boxes was available also and could be glued or tacked into layers to make decorative comb cases, hanging wall shelves, miniature furniture, match safes, spice boxes, picture or mirror frames. Occasionally, large pieces of furniture such as a bed, table, or chest were covered with chip-carved panels made of layers of wood from cigar boxes. Applied geometric forms dominated, with triangles, squares, and circles. Scraps of glass might be incorporated in the design, or mismatched knobs might be utilized.

Around the "Roaring Twenties"

Bride's box, 18″ wide, 10¼″ deep, 7″ high, **$1,100.** Iowa.

Modified buttocks basket, 10″ wide, 9″ deep, 9″ high, **$100.** Ohio.

Wall or one-half splint basket, 10″ wide, 5″ deep, 6¼″ high, **$55.** Illinois.

One-half-bushel basket, eastern New England, **$95.** Wisconsin.

Hickory splint vegetable basket, circa 1890, 16″ square, 16½″ high, **$45.** Alabama.

Splint gathering basket, 23″ wide, 17″ deep, 14″ high, **$75.** Illinois.

Reed basket, 15½″ wide, 13″ deep, 14″ high, **$40.** Illinois.

Splint cotton carrying basket, 22″ diameter, 20″ high, **$75.** Alabama.

Splint gathering basket from the North Carolina mountains, 13″ wide, 9½″ deep, 8″ high, **$55.** Alabama.

cigarettes replaced cigars in popularity and fewer boxes were available. Later, wooden boxes gave way to stout cardboard containers. Thus, the basic raw material for tramp art was lacking. These curios, frequently constructed by men on the move, but not by hobos as such, became collectible as interest in American folk art developed. Tramp art's lifespan roughly covered the last half of the 1800s through the first two decades of the 1900s.

A folk art medicine cabinet is made from boxes, but it lacks the chip carving characteristic of tramp art. Its decorations depend on incised lines (cut into the surface) and loops rather than notches.

Take some shells, a bit of mirror, a picture of a pretty girl, tiny pieces of glass, and go creative. The folk art shelf shown has these aspects. Shells form the center of the red glass flowers with their leaves of green glass or carved wood. Women of the last half of the 1800s enjoyed doing craft projects similar to this.

Currently, children, as a club project, glue macaroni in shells, tubular forms, or other shapes onto backgrounds. Sprayed with colored paint, these bright gifts are offered to their moms. In the 1850s to the late 1800s, ladies created entire pictures with real shells. *Godey's Lady's Book,* a magazine founded in 1830 by Louis Antoine Godey and the first such publication in the United States, influenced the tastes of thousands of women. Its format featured personal as well as home fashions and frequently included directions for fanciful projects such as shell work. For a slight fee, the magazine could supply the necessary shells. The frame shown utilizes these seashore patterns. It probably dates to around 1880.

In Pennsylvania, flat yet colorful

Tramp art picture frames, 13″ wide at base, 23″ high, **$165.** Iowa.

Medicine cabinet, 17½″ wide, 6″ deep, 25″ high, **$180.** Ohio.

Hand-carved hanging shelf with shell and glass ornamentation, 9½″ wide, 6¼″ deep, 23″ high, **$85.** Iowa.

Oval shell frame, circa 1880, 13″ wide, 21½″ high, **$45.** Iowa.

angels, birds, hearts, and flowers adorned the certificates of birth and baptism that colonists of German extraction hung on their walls. Those with artistic hand lettering, written in German, were used until about 1800. Wedding certificates, sheet music, hymnals, and Bibles also were accented with watercolor decorations. In the early 1800s, records containing vital statistics no longer were hand done. Instead, printed forms that could be filled in with the proper names and dates were available. The stiff figures on them were still hand colored, however, and the German language, not English, continued in use. This custom declined after about 1840.

It was in derision, not as a compliment, that the "shadow" pictures so popular in the 1700s came to be termed silhouettes. King Louis XV occupied the French throne from 1715–1774. For a short period of time, Etienne de Silhouette (1709–1767) was his penny-squeezing Minister of Finance. The non-parsimonious nobility ridiculed his economical policies, they dubbed anything cheap "a la Silhouette." Since this official enjoyed cutting out profile portraits of people that were less expensive than oil paintings, the nobles found this art form amusing and too common to suit their expensive tastes. They referred to them as silhouettes, and the name stuck.

There were two main types. Hollow cuts, the more common, were completed with the aid of a machine that reduced the size of the shadow cast on a sheet of paper by a person's profile. This could be traced and cut out. The white paper frame was preserved and mounted on a dark background to show off the profile.

Another kind was completed when the artist took black paper, looked at the subject and, working rapidly with scissors, cut out the outline of his bust

Fractur dated 1813, 15¼″ wide, 18½″ high, **$100.** Ohio.

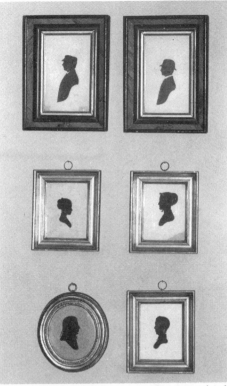

Silhouettes: top pair, 7″ wide, 9½″ high, **$150** each. Middle pair, **$125** each. Bottom right, **$125.** Bottom left is not old. Indiana.

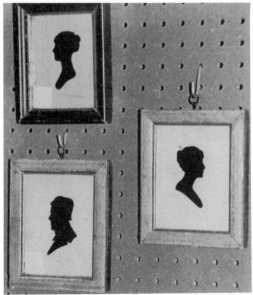

Hollow-cut silhouettes; top left: Faith Holms, 5¼″ wide, 6¼″ high, **$160.** Bottom left: John C. Clark, 5¼″ wide, 6¼″ high. Bottom right: Patience H. Adams, 5¼″ wide and 6¼″ high, **$345** the pair. Georgia.

Black on white silhouette, 12¼″ wide, 14½″ high, **$195.** Iowa.

Black on white silhouette, 12″ wide, 14½″ high, **$175.** Iowa.

Black on white silhouette, 12″ wide, 14½″ high, **$175.** Iowa.

or figure by hand. This solid piece was affixed to a light background to create the almost shadowlike appearance.

Sometimes, an outline drawing in black will be called a silhouette. Objects such as leaves can also be traced around to form such dark pictures. Gilding or a bit of touching up with ink or watercolors added ornamentation.

Amateurs enjoyed creating silhouettes, but the rich and royal sought the best "shade cutters" in England, France, and Germany in the days when this inexpensive substitute for oil painting was popular. In the United States, the well-known artist, Charles Willson Peale executed hollow-cut busts. He worked in the late 1700s and early 1800s, and President George Washington posed for him in 1794.

A Frenchman, Augustin Edouart, traversed this country in the 1840s cutting full-length outlines, usually mounted against sepia or lithographed backgrounds. This artist sometimes penciled in clothing details or hair, and his hand with the scissors was quick and sure. Edouart made a duplicate as he worked, preserving a record of his artistry. While he signed his efforts A E at times, he usually employed a more complete signature. Many famous Americans posed for him, but he was not averse to representing a family grouping in this shadowy manner.

William Henry Brown (1808–1883) of Charleston, South Carolina, cut free-hand, usually full-length silhouettes, frequently set against lithographed backgrounds. These might have touches of gilding and white paint. Twenty-seven portraits of "Distinguished American Citizens" were presented in a book with that title. The statesman-orator Daniel Webster, presidents of the nation, and the "Great Compromiser" Henry Clay were among those represented. It is difficult to separate Brown's book lithographs of 1845 from later examples published in the 1930s. While Brown's works are scarce, it is still possible to find some by Edouart. Silhouettes gradually lost their popular status after 1839 when Louis J. M. Daguerre, a Frenchman, developed a photographic technique with prints which he termed daguerreotypes. Costumes and hairstyles of the past can be duplicated, but when combined with aging paper, glass with bubbles or waves, and old frames, the silhouettes have the characteristics of vintage examples.

Pick a portrait or a picture. Are the people's shoulders hunched unnaturally? Do the proportions of the anatomy appear distorted? Are the figures squat and stilted? Does the composition appear flat, without depth? Problems of perspective, background, and dimensions are difficult for an untrained painter to solve. Round objects seem especially hard to depict. If the artist had trouble sketching hands, this portion of the body might be concealed with a draped scarf or flowers. Frequently, a farm fowl may be larger than nearby human beings or a building. A drawing might be done on anything that was handy, including a spare board. The term folk art is applied to such artistic efforts.

Pictures of unknown vintage can, on occasion, be dated by the type of garments the individuals wear, hairstyles, or foot gear. It is more difficult to classify scenes as to time unless an easy-to-date item such as an old automobile or locomotive is shown. Style, paint, techniques, and the canvas used may provide age clues. Since folk art has revived in popularity, people are purchasing "ancestral" portraits to adopt for their homes. If you have likenesses of your ancestors, now is the time to hang them.

Oil painting on academy board of George Washington, circa 1880, 27" wide, 31" high, **$350.** Iowa.

Primitive painting, circa 1830, 10¾" wide, 13" high, **$1,250.** Georgia.

239

Primitive painting, circa 1850, in 22k gold frame, 33½″ wide, 44″ high, **$2,200.** Georgia.

Oil painting, circa 1850, 20″ wide, 24″ high, **$600.** Iowa.

12 Nautical lore and treasures

According to Mark Twain in his book *Life on the Mississippi,* "Ya egg suckin', sheep stealin', one-eyed son of a stuffed monkey," was supposedly an insult hurled at steamship crew members by backwoods rafters. They had no lights at night and were afraid the large craft would run them down in the dark.

Presently, as a safety measure, lights are required on vessels that operate at night. In the late 1800s, kerosene lamps were offered in catalogs in either zinc or brass,

Pair of running lights made by Perkins Marine Lamp & Home Corp., Brooklyn, N.Y., U.S.A., 12" high, **$115** each. Iowa.

Running lights, left: 11″ high, **$75.** Right: 12½″ high, **$75.** Iowa.

Steamboat running light, made by Wilcox, Krittenden & Co., Inc., **$150.** Iowa.

Brass steamboat whistle from Minnie Snyder, 23½″ high, **$300.** Iowa.

and most were manufactured on the East Coast. On most riverboats, two running lights were mandatory at the front, one red and one green. This told other vessels which side was near because one color always lighted the starboard (right-hand side of the ship as one faces forward toward the bow), and the other light was hung on the port side or left. A larger vessel required bigger lights. At times, only one lamp with a combination red and green light would be sufficient if the boat were small.

The larger running lights are rarer. The example pictured next came from a steamboat, is green, and was made in Middleton, Connecticut, by Wilcox, Krittenden & Co., Inc.

Excitement was generated when a grand steamboat approached a town, its whistle (pulled by a cord or treadle operated) blasting out a salute. Boys rushed to the landing, and many a lad dreamed of growing up to be a strutting riverboat pilot. On inland waterways, the pilot ranked above the captain, who functioned more as a business manager. This differs from the system on ocean-going vessels where the captain is the highest official. Pilots had to know the waters on which they navigated. Each year, they were required to turn in their licenses and were issued new ones. This greatly restricts the number available to collectors. An apprentice was required to sketch the entire river if he desired to pass a test that qualified him to navigate the whole length. This was only one of the requirements. It was possible to be assigned a specific stretch of water, and the pilot could only navigate there. A skilled pilot for an area where there were rapids was of more value than the ordinary ones who received the fabulous wage of one hundred dollars a day at a time when most people labored for a few dollars per week. The rapids pilot took over to guide the boat safely through churning

Ship's wheel from a tugboat marked "John Hastie & Co. Ltd., Greenock" is 36″ in diameter, **$625.** Louisiana.

Brass course corrector, 10″ diameter, **$125.** Louisiana.

Oak map box in which map rolled to show the location in the course of the river, 17″ wide, 13½″ deep, 6″ high. Museum quality. Iowa.

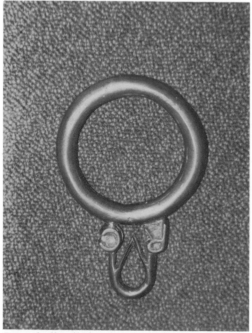

Brass bellpull that was attached to the end of a pullcord in the pilot's house to ring the engine room, 5″ diameter, **$65.** Iowa.

danger spots. For example, with its rapids, the section between LeClaire, Iowa, and Davenport was difficult to maneuver. Special pilots could sign up with a packet company for freelance or combine both. Some went from Le-Claire to Davenport and back by buggy to await the next boat. Others did the reverse. Because their knowledge and skill was essential, these men could amass great wealth. There is a legend that pilots congregated and chatted in the shade of a huge tree in LeClaire as they awaited assignments. This became known as "The Green Tree."

Wheels from steamboat pilot houses were wooden, some as large as ten feet in diameter. This makes them too large to display in most homes, but some restaurants can accommodate them in their decor.

Maps were used, but an oak box in which to store and see them is a rare, museum-quality find. The map needed could be attached to two rollers so that a specified location on the river could be seen through the box's glass top and could be turned when that area was passed. Additional maps were kept behind a base door that dropped open. These could be placed on the rollers as desired. A course corrector with dials that showed bearings was an additional navigation aid on some vessels.

The pilot was responsible for telling the engineer down in the engine room what to do; for example, when he could use more steam and increase the speed. A brass bell with a pull wire (generally not a rope) was mounted on or near the ceiling of the engine room. The wire continued up to the pilot house where there usually was a custom-cast brass bell pull, a sort of river folk art item. It might bear the initials of the boat. A certain number of tugs on the wire

clanged the bell to signal and direct the engineer's activities. The gong shown in the picture was retrieved from the Mississippi River boat *The Quinlan.*

The engineer kept his eyes on a steam gauge. The one illustrated was made by the Sterling Company, Chicago, Illinois. Some people remove the centers, preserve the brass frames, and mount clocks in them. This reduces their value.

There are stories about races on the river when one boat challenged another, and this could cause disastrous results. If a pilot wasn't on the alert, it was always possible to run up on a sandbar since the river constantly changed. For this reason the boats had shallow, flat bottoms to work their way off such obstructions. Another danger was the possibility of an explosion. At one time, there were no laws establishing safety measures, and life preservers were not available. Instead, the wooden doors

Brass engine room bell, 12″ diameter, **$175.** Iowa.

Brass steam gauge from engine room, 14¼″ diameter, **$145.** Iowa.

Wooden lifeboard, 12″ wide, 1¾″ deep, 48″ high. Museum quality. Iowa.

Excursion posters circa 1920 are difficult to find as most were torn down and discarded. **$85** to **$100** each. Iowa.

and shutters on the boats were hung on hinges. They could be pulled off easily to form floating devices if the boat was sinking. In some cases, pine planks with cutout hand grips served as life boards on which people could lie when it was necessary to abandon a boat. A man who is steeped in river traditions found such a board in an antique shop, and he was the only one who recognized what it was. It was marked *STR* (Steamer) *City of Baton Rouge,* and since it is such an unusual item, it is included for its interest only. Later, cork life jackets were placed on board. Because boat engines were extremely costly, they were salvaged whenever possible and reused in another vessel.

Furnishings were as elaborate as the vessel itself. A high-class excursion boat of the mid- to late 1800s would have ornate accommodations that included the finest Victorian furniture. China and silver that once graced the festive tables are rarely found today and can only be authenticated when they are marked with the name of the steamboat. While glamor was everywhere, sanitation was primitive on early riverboats. Debris was cast off on one side of the vessel, and the water supply was drawn up from the opposite side.

It is said that the first excursion on the Mississippi was sponsored by a church group. When there were conventions, one of the pleasurable events often scheduled was a ride on a riverboat. Paper memorabilia, including posters and tickets, attracts collectors. Some enjoy sheet music from the past.

It is difficult to find riverboat passes that formerly were exchanged by presidents of each line and also given to the presidents of various railroads. These were issued in the bearer's name. When the head of a steamship line desired to travel, he sent passes to all the head executives of the railroads on his intended route. He received train passes in ex-

Steamboat tickets, **$10** to **$20** each depending on size and condition. Iowa.

change and could travel free. Today, boat passes are rarer than those from railroads. Postcards from the past that show river transportation or double cards, which when viewed through a stereoscope, take on a three-dimensional look, are sought. Catalogs provide enjoyment to many.

Nautical articles on inland waterways did not have to be constructed of brass, but those on the sea did because salt corrodes other metals. For example, the captain's telescope illustrated is of brass. Another one for an ocean-going ship was made in France and has its own case. Binoculars were available in brass.

A holder where a ship's captain could place his pocket watch at night for safe keeping was carved from wood and included a glass-enclosed drawing of a sailing vessel. It is inscribed on the back "Grandfather Capt. Figges from a Sea Capt. Gloucester, Mass. E. A. Hooper." Both the ocean and inland rivers rate an important place in the history of the United States.

The presence of country-type memorabilia and folk art helps reincarnate a visual, tangible picture of the past. The itinerate cobbler who lived in the early 1800s sat on his tool bench as he worked. He split the wood for square little pegs and cut the leather for boots from the hide saved from the steer the farmer butchered in the fall for the family's meat supply. A lad took out his Noah's Ark, a Sunday toy, when reverence for the Sabbath Day confined him to religiously oriented play and he was not allowed to indulge in boisterous activities. A bonnet-wearing Shaker lady can be depicted as one sits in the plain, yet beautiful, chair designed and manufactured by this religious sect who felt work and worship of God were united. Your home is all your own when you establish a country and folk art decor. The pieces are already scarred, but mellowed from use; and it is to be anticipated their value will increase as the years pass. Valuable, useful, unique — that's a combination hard to beat.

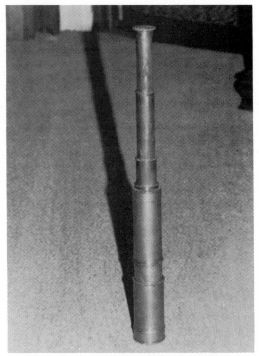

Nautical brass telescope; compressed size 9¾"; extended, 32½", **$180.** Iowa.

Sheet music with river theme, **$5** to **$15.** "*Steamboat Bill*" was priced at **$15** at the Steamboat Convention. Iowa.

Moravian table with shoe feet, no nails or screws, can be disassembled for easy moving, dated on storage compartment beneath top, "May 10, 1713," and is 38″ wide, 58½″ long, 31½″ high, **$5,000.** Pewter candlesticks on table, 7″ high, **$300** a pair. Trenchers or wooden plates, 7″ diameter to 8½″ diameter, **$165** each. Wooden serving bowls, **$65** each. Iowa.

▷ Lion coffee box, 21″ wide, 21″ deep, 27″ high at the front, 32″ high at the back, **$225.** Wooden sled made by Reeser, 1888, 15″ wide, 9″ high, 31″ long, **$145.** Spinning wheel, **$350.** Hand-carved wooden goose, 19″ long, 14″ tall, **$145.** Iowa.

▽ *Below:* pine settee, often called deacon's bench, 60″ wide, 15″ deep, 32½″ high, **$650.** Quilt on bench, 69½″ × 58″, **$85.** Six-legged pine bench in foreground, **$225.** Nebraska.

◁ Totem poles found around an Indian lodge, circa 1900, 6½″ high, **$1,000** each. North Carolina.

▽ *Below, quilts on left frame:* top left: twin size by Molly Long, Prosperity, South Carolina, variation of Irish Chain, circa 1890, **$185.** Top right: double size by Matt Wise, Prosperity, South Carolina, double circled star, circa 1890, **$185.** Bottom: queen size by Molly Long, paddle wheel and wheel of fortune variation, circa 1870. **$300.** *Quilts on middle frame:* top left: variation of Orange Peel and Rob Peter to Pay Paul, circa 1890, **$225.** Top right: pattern unnamed, Midwestern origin, circa 1920, **$125.** Bottom: crazy quilt that spans fifty years of fabric use, 1840 to 1890, **$250.** *Quilt on right frame:* Variable Star, never washed, circa 1870, South Carolina, **$325.** Frame with triangles in a circle by Matt Wise, circa 1890, **$30.** Georgia.

▷Coverlet mentioned in 1820 Canadian will, needs some repair, **$200.** Duck decoy with glass eyes, 17″ long, **$90.** Small grained box, 18″ wide, 10″ deep, 9″ high, circa 1800, **$485.** Large grained box, 28¾″ wide, 13¼″ deep, 11″ high, **$525.** Tennessee.

▽*Below:* Whirligig, man sawing wood, early twentieth century, 22″ × 27″, **$165.** Ohio.

◁Open cupboard, pine, Georgia origin, 33½″ wide, 17″ deep, 72″ high, **$695.** Spongeware spittoon on top shelf, **$95.** Blue-and-white spongeware bean pot on second shelf, **$145.** Blue-and-white bowl on bottom shelf, **$65.** Georgia.

▽*Below:* Amish coverlet woven by William Nye of Lebanon County, Pennsylvania, **$695.** Pine kneeling bench, **$195.** Red painted sled signed P. Larrwurz, **$350.** Wooden mortar and pestle, **$95.** Sampler, Joan Carpenter, age thirteen, not dated, **$225.** Tennessee.

▷ Cannonball rope bed, pine head- and footboards, maple posts, circa 1830, 50½″ wide, 83″ long, 45½″ high, **$475.** Covering the bed is a Dunkard friendship quilt, 74¼″×72″. Embroidered in quilt squares are common Dunkard names— Miller, Brubaker, Garber, Denlinger, Mama (the grandmother), and Mother (the mother). Quilt was a pre-wedding gift to the bride-to-be, **$250.** Duck decoy in window, early twentieth century, **$45.** Blanket chest at foot of bed, 44″ wide, 19½″ deep, 23¼″ high, **$350.** Ohio.

▷ Closed, two-piece cupboard, original blue-gray paint; base 39½″ wide, 17½″ deep, 30″ high; top 13″ deep, 46″ high, **$950.** It contains collection of toy animals made either of wood, composition, or hide, and some nodders. On the top shelf is a large, hide-covered cow with bellow; head tilts and moos, late 1800s, **$250.** Ohio.

◁Pie cupboard with pierced tin front and sides, 42½″ wide, 17″ deep, 52¼″ high, **$395**. Georgia quilt, circa 1910, 65½″×87½″, **$145**. Armless, slat-back Shaker rocker with re- placed rockers, **$48**. Georgia.

◁*Left screen:* two copper pans, **$95** each. Long- handled brass pan, **$47**. Butter knife, **$42**. *Right screen:* copper ladle, **$42**. Yarn winder, **$32**. Bread- board, **$31**. Walnut spoon, **$45**. Tobacco cutter, **$32**. Brass pan, **$55**. On floor in front of screen, copper pan with iron handle, **$145**. Nebraska.

Opposite page: open cupboard, original red paint, snipe hinges, **$1,200.** Iowa. Lighting devices and Shaker boxes in open cupboard are identified from left to right and from top to bottom.

Hanging on beam above cupboard: circular candle mold, 6″ diameter, 11″ high, **$400.** Tin lantern, early 1800s, 13″ high, **$185.** Wooden crusie, rare, unpriced, 10½″ high; punched tin lantern, 10½″ high, **$165.** Punched tin lantern (erroneously called Paul Revere), 10½″ high, **$165.** Wooden lantern with heart openings, rare, unpriced, 10½″ high. Punched tin lantern, 14″ high, **$165.**

Top shelf: freestanding tin candle box, tole, brass knob, 9½″ long, 5″ deep, 5″ high, **$195.** Hourglass, tiger maple, early 1800s, 7″ high, **$700.** Tole box, 2¾″ wide, 2″ deep, 1¾″ high, **$65.** Tea canister, tole with asphaltum finish 4¼″ diameter, 8″ high, **$125.** Syrup pitcher, tole with asphaltum finish, 4¼″ diameter, 4½″ high, **$195.**

Second shelf: collapsible miner's lantern (partly obscured), tole, patented Jan. 24, 1865, **$95.** Whale oil lamp, brass, 6″ high, **$145.** Tinder lighter, pistol type, iron, 8″ long, 4″ high, **$400.** Double whale oil, sickroom or nurse's lamp, has tole pan inside used to heat liquid, 4½″

diameter, 8″ high, **$165.** Make-do or made-up lamp of pewter on wood with rotten candle made from old fat, circa 1800, 3″ square, 5″ high, **$110.** Old candle valued at **$16.** Tole tinder box with striker, tinder, candle to light, 4″ diameter, 3″ high, **$325.**

Third shelf: wedding band, hog scraper, ejector candlestick (called wedding band because of the brass band encircling the stem), 8″ high, **$400.** Betty lamp, 6″ high, **$110.** Spiral candlestick, wooden base, 8″ high, **$210.**

Bottom shelf: the three lighting devices in front include rush light, iron, wooden base, with piece of rush attached, 8½″ high, **$250.** Betty lamp stand or tidy top, 6½″ high, **$110.** Betty lamp on top of stand, **$135.** Tin double whale oil petticoat lamp can be used flat on table, on chair finial (it has a round, cylindrical channel in its base), or on a candlestick, 4¼″ high, **$85.** Shaker boxes, priced by sizes, **$200** to **$275** each.

Wall area to right of cupboard: cathedral base candle molds, eight-candle, twelve-candle, **$165.** Single molds, 21″ high, **$175.** Single mold, 15½″ high, **$165.** Double crusie or Phoebe, **$250.** Sugar nipper or cutter, 9″, **$65.** Sugar nipper, 7″, **$65.** Copper pans, 11″ and 9″ in diameter, **$145** each.

Captain's telescope and case made in France, collapsed size 10", extended 29½", **$150.** Iowa.

Ship captain's watch holder from a sea captain in Gloucester, Massachusetts, 2½" wide, 9¼" high, **$250.** Iowa.

Brass nautical binoculars, 7" high, **$120.** Iowa.

Brass ship's bell from small launch, 6½" diameter, **$155.** Iowa.

Brass propellers, 11″ and 15″, **$25** and **$40.** Iowa.

Rock anchor, 24″ long, 15″ from fluke to fluke. The fluke is the triangular pointed end of an anchor arm by which the anchor catches in the ground. **$35.** Iowa.

Bibliography

Andrews, Edward Deming and Faith. *Work and Worship: The Economic Order of the Shakers.* Greenwich, Conn.: New York Graphic Society, 1974.

Art & Antiques. *Americana: Folk and Decorative Art.* New York: Art & Antiques, 1982.

Fales, Dean A., Jr., and Bishop, Robert. *American Painted Furniture 1660–1880.* New York: E. P. Dutton, 1979.

Fendelman, Helaine. *Tramp Art: An Itinerant's Folk Art.* New York: E. P. Dutton, 1975.

Gould, Mary Earle. *Antique Tin & Tole Ware: Its History and Romance.* Rutland, Vt.: Charles E. Tuttle Co., 1969.

———. *Early American Wooden Ware.* Rutland, Vt.: Charles E. Tuttle Co., 1979.

Hayward, Arthur H. *Colonial and Early American Lighting.* New York: Dover Publications, Inc., 1962.

Heisey, John W. *A Checklist of American Coverlet Weavers.* Williamsburg, Virg.: The Colonial Williamsburg Foundation, 1978.

Jackson, Mrs. E. Neville. *Silhouettes: A History and Dictionary of Artists.* New York: Dover Publications, Inc., 1981.

Montgomery, Pauline. *Indiana Coverlet Weavers and Their Coverlets.* Indianapolis: Hoosier Heritage Press, 1974.

Perry, Evan. *Collecting Antique Metalware.* Garden City, N.Y.: Doubleday & Company, Inc., 1974.

Revi, Albert Christian. *The Spinning Wheel's Complete Book of Antiques.* New York: Grosset & Dunlap, 1977.

Rushlight Club. *Early Lighting.* The Rushlight Club: 1979.

Safford, Carleton L., and Bishop, Robert. *America's Quilts and Coverlets.* New York: E. P. Dutton, 1980.

Shea, John G. *The American Shakers and Their Furniture.* New York: Van Nostrand Reinhold Co., 1971.

Swedberg, Robert and Harriett. *Country Pine Furniture, Styles and Prices.* Des Moines, Iowa: Wallace-Homestead Book Co., 1980.

Teleki, Gloria Roth. *The Baskets of Rural America.* New York: E. P. Dutton, 1975.

Thwing, Leroy. *Flickering Flames.* Rutland, Vt.: Charles E. Tuttle Co., 1963.

Webster, Donald Blake. *Decorated Stoneware Pottery of North America.* Rutland, Vt.: Charles E. Tuttle Co., 1980.

Glossary

Apron A piece that hides the construction details on chairs, tables, and case pieces. It's beneath the top of a table, under the seat of a chair, and between the legs of dressers, cabinets, or cupboards.

Andirons Ornamental supports for logs in a fireplace.

Apothecary chest A druggist's pharmaceutical storage unit with many drawers in a wooden frame.

Arrow back Back spindles on settees or chairs that bear a resemblance to arrows.

Asphaltum A brownish black coating of mineral asphalt in varnish applied on tin to resemble oriental lacquer work.

Bandbox Cardboard or hand-sawed bentwood box covered with bright-colored paper, used for storage or travel in the late 1700s through about 1845.

Bas-relief A molding or carving that projects above the background.

Bellows Apparatus that blows out a stream of air through a narrow tube when its sides are pressed together. Often used to make a fire burn brightly.

Bennington Ceramic ware signed or documented by one of the two potteries that operated in Bennington, Vermont, in the 1800s.

Berlin work Frequently refers to a type of needlework (also called worsted work) where perforated designs on cardboard were worked with large stitches and brightly colored thick wool threads to make a picture with sentimental expressions such as "Remember Me" or "Home Sweet Home."

Betty lamp Simple grease or oil burning lamp with a built-in tube in which the wick was held and elevated.

Bird roaster Small reflector-type oven (usually tin) in which a plucked and cleaned bird was hooked for cooking at the fireplace.

Boston rocker Spindle-back rocking chair with a solid wooden seat that curves up at the rear and under in front. Originally painted and decorated.

Bottle jack A mechanical spit that vaguely resembles a bottle. When the spring-operated mechanism was wound, it rotated slowly to permit meat to cook evenly over the flames in a fireplace.

Bride's box Brightly decorated oval box constructed of thin wood, traditionally made by a groom for his bride to carry her delicate, treasured possessions to her new home.

Bucket bench A shelf structure, either closed or open, on which water buckets were kept.

Bureau commode Three-drawer chest, with or without towel bars, used to hold personal cleansing supplies in pre-plumbing days.

Burl A diseased hump on a tree. Its decorative pattern could be used to form bowls, butter paddles, or could be sliced for ornamental furniture veneer.

Burning fluid A combination of alcohol and turpentine (camphine) used in lamps about 1830, but so highly explosive that its use was discontinued around 1850.

Busks Decorated stays that slipped into elongated pockets in a woman's dress to provide abdominal support.

Butt joint The flat ends of two boards attached with no overlap to form the simplest of joints.

Butter mold Butter was packed into a wooden mold to form it into one-fourth to two-pound sizes. Most left a decorative pattern on top including floral designs, animals, nuts, fruits, or fowl.

Butter worker A device used in making butter by forcing the liquid out of the globulas. It could be a wooden frame on legs with a roller or merely a small paddle-like wooden object used in a bowl with a drain. The paddle was pressed against the butter to squeeze the moisture out.

Camphine Turpentine alone. A few lamps were made to burn a turpentine-alcohol mixture called camphine (frequently spelled camphene).

Candle box Box that hung on the wall or laid flat to hold extra candles.

Cast iron Molten iron poured into molds to solidify into shape.

Chamber stick A saucer-type candleholder, usually with a finger loop, used to light the way to the bedchamber at night.

Cheese press Press with a screwing device used to squeeze liquid out of cheese when it is being made.

Commode washstand An enclosed cupboard where supplies for personal cleansing were kept in the days before plumbing.

Country furniture Articles with a rustic flavor frequently made at home by hand out of native woods by non-professionals.

Coverlet Handwoven spreads for beds with designs and fancy names. Made from colonial days on, their popularity gradually declined by around the late 1860s. The four main types were double weave, overshot, summer, and winter. (See each type by name.) Before the Jacquard loom was invented in 1801, small looms wove coverlets in two or perhaps three pieces that were then seamed together.

Crimper Pastry tool used to decorate and seal the edges of a piecrust and cut off excess dough. Sometimes used to cut out cookies.

Crusie A simple lamp with a channel for the wick. Grease was the usual fuel.

Double-weave coverlet Two warps and woofs handwoven and joined with some openings in between to form a sort of pocket, which can be pulled apart gently. Geometrical pattern usually has seam where two pieces were sewn together to form this bed cover. *See* Coverlet.

Dry sink Cupboard with tray or well that was usually zinc lined. Used in the kitchen when water was carried, not piped, into the house.

Farrier Blacksmith, someone who shoes horses.

Fire back Metal, ornamental sheet placed against the back of the chimney opening to protect the wall from heat and to reflect warmth.

Firkin A one-fourth bushel measure or a small wooden container for lard, butter, or other items.

Fluke Triangular, pointed end of an anchor that catches in the ground.

Folk art Part of a country's heritage which shows people's attempts to express themselves even though they may lack training in art. Some folk art is utilitarian, others ornamental.

Footman An English term for a four-legged fireplace stand for pots, pans, and kettles. *Also see* Quad.

Footwarmer A portable stove used to keep feet warm in wagons, carriages, or unheated buildings and churches.

Fraktur A certificate of birth or baptism written in German with embellished letters and decorated with colorful angels, birds, or flowers. These were hung on walls in the homes of Pennsylvania Germans. Weddings, sheet music, hymnals, and also Bibles could be illuminated in this manner.

Gesso A mixture of plaster-of-paris and glue that was poured into molds and, when set, carved, painted, or gilded.

Gimbal lantern A lamp mounted in a bracket that permits the lamp to remain level. Often, gimbal lamps were used on ships. When the ship rolled, they remained horizontal.

Gooseneck A spout in a kettle that resembles a goose's neck.

Graining Paint usually applied to represent the grain of a specific wood. Some is fanciful, however.

Hitchcock From about 1820 to the 1850s, Lambert Hitchcock made painted and decorated chairs similar to Sheraton fancy chairs. Other companies made them also, but the generic name is Hitchcock.

Hogscraper candlestick A candleholder with a double purpose. Its cupped metal end could be used to scrape the bristles off a scalded hog at butchering time. At other times, it sat upright and the socket held a candle.

Hollow-cut silhouette The outline of a person's profile is cut from white paper and the frame, not the solid piece, is retained. This frame is mounted on black paper and the resulting silhouette shows a person's bust or entire figure. It is almost like the print of a shadow. *See* Silhouette.

Incised A design cut or engraved in a surface.

Insinglass *See* Mica.

Jacquard coverlets Were made on a loom invented by Joseph Jacquard that used a series of punched cards similar to a player piano's music rolls, which controlled the design. While it was hand-operated, it had a flying shuttle. Skilled weavers could make one-piece coverlets with complex patterns in one day. Elaborate borders might have the weaver's name, state, date, and the customer's name at the corner. *See also* Coverlet.

Japanning Lacquer work originating in the Orient, used on wood or tin. It was decorative and artistic. *See* Asphaltum and Tole.

Jelly cupboard A small, closed, kitchen cupboard, with perhaps two drawers, used for storing jellies, jams, and various articles.

Knife box Usually a low, lidless, two-division, portable container with a handle at the top used to hold cutlery. Most are made of wood, but occasionally one in tin is found.

Lift-top commode A cupboard with a lift lid in which a wash bowl and pitcher for personal cleansing were placed.

Mercury glass When a silver solution was put between two layers of blown glass, silvered or mercury glass resulted.

Mica Minerals that crystallize in thin, often translucent layers that resist heat and electricity. Thin sheets of transparent mica are often called isinglass.

Milk paint Paint that has a milk base with pigments and drying ingredients added. Homemade in the 1800s, commonly in red, gray, or blue.

Mourning picture In-memorial themes were stamped on a paper background and embroidered with floss. Hands, feet, and faces were painted in. This idea was an English import that lasted throughout the 1800s.

Noggin Wooden pitcher, handle and all, carved from one piece of wood.

Open cupboard A cupboard with no doors on the top.

Overshot coverlet A handwoven spread for a bed, usually made in a geometric pattern. Stitches skipped over the top produce a bumpy look and feel. A flatter, tighter design results when there are no long skips. It is generally woven in two, and occasionally three pieces, which are seamed together. *See* Coverlet.

Peg lamp A link between a candle and a lamp. A prong (peg or stump) extended down to the center of the font (fuel holder) to fit into the socket of a candlestick to form a lamp.

Pegged construction Instead of nails or screws, wooden pins or dowels (pegs) are used as fasteners. Handmade pegs are irregular in size and shape and appear slightly squarish. They are not perfectly round as modern machine-made dowels are.

Penny foot Rounded foot in penny shape on the end of a fireplace trivet.

Petticoat lamp Small lamp that flares out at the base.

Pewter Not a mined metal, but an alloy consisting mainly of tin, combined with copper, lead, antimony, and occasionally bismuth.

Pie safe A closed cupboard with pierced tin panels where baked goods could be stored. The punched holes let air in to help prevent molding, but kept out rodents and flies. Screening or pierced boards also could be used.

Pierced tin lantern A portable, outdoor light with a pierced tin frame to give the candle air while protecting it from drafts and to let a feeble light shine out.

Piggin Small wooden bucket with one stave extended to form a handle so it could be hung on a wall.

Pricket Early candleholder with a sharp prong that speared the candle to hold it erect. It predates the socket type in which the candle sits in a surrounding frame.

Quad A four-legged fireplace stand for pots, pans, or kettles similar to a trivet (three legs.) In England, it may be called a footman.

Relief *See* Bas-relief.

Repro or reproduction A copy or imitation. Reproductions are not fraudulent unless they are misrepresented as the genuine article.

Rockingham Earthenware with a mottled dark brown or deep brown glaze first produced in England in 1745 on the estate of the Marquis de Rockingham. Made at Bennington, Vermont, prior to the mid-1800s and by other American potteries.

Rush A marsh plant used to make woven seats. Rolled paper is frequently used now.

Rush light Made from rush, a marsh plant. The core was dried, soaked in grease, tallow, or animal fat, which was allowed to harden. It was suspended at a forty-five degree angle in a metal holder, and lighted for an early-type, smoky illumination.

Saltbox A container for coarse salt. Some types hung on the wall.

Salt glaze A hard, glossy surface on stoneware produced by throwing ordinary salt into the kiln (oven) when the temperature within reached about 2300 degrees Farenheit so that it would vaporize. If particles of salt hit the clay, some pitting resulted.

Scouring box A wooden, wall-hanging board with a container to hold ashes or pummice and a place to scour knives.

Settle A wooden, high-backed settee with solid sides that protected the sitter from drafts.

Sewing bird A brass or iron device screwed to a tabletop to hold cloth in the bird's beak while sewing.

Silhouette A picture in outline form, especially a profile portrait. It can be cut from black paper and placed on a light background. It has a shadowlike appearance. For another type, *see* Hollow-cut silhouette.

Six-board chest A simple, boxlike structure made from six pieces of wood butted together, with a hinged top, a bottom, and four sides.

Springerle A rolling pin or cookie board carved with designs of animals, birds, people, boats, or other subject matter to make thin cookies with patterns. These were called springerle cookies.

Sparking lamp Supposedly, a small lamp was lighted when a suitor called on a young lady. When it burned down, it was time for the young man to leave. None of the lighting books consulted confirmed this tale.

Spur A projection on a candlestick that permitted it to hang on the back of a chair or on a loom.

Sticking tommy A miner's candleholder with a prong that he could push into a beam so his hands would be free to work.

Stoneware Ceramic (clay) product, which is non-porous, with a vitreous (glasslike) surface. It is hard paste (can scratch iron). Jugs, jars, and crocks are examples of stoneware.

Student lamp Has a projecting arm for the burner that is lower than the container for the kerosene.

Summer and winter coverlet Has a reverse pattern on the back. For example, the front has a light design against a dark background and when turned over, the background is light while the design is dark. It is not heavy and can be used at any season. It usually is woven in two parts so it has a seam. Geometrical patterns prevail. *Also see* Coverlet.

Tape Strips of colored fabric used by Shaker sisters to weave chair seats or backs.

Theorem A stencil used to paint designs on velvet, but occasionally used on silk or satin. Paper ones were also made. A combination of stencils was needed to form complicated patterns.

Tinder box A metal box that held supplies to make a fire: candle stubs, inflammable material called tinder, and a piece of steel and flint. Sparks produced when the latter two were struck together fell into the tinder (cotton or linen cloth) and caught fire. The candle was lit and from it a fire could be started.

Tole Tinware, frequently painted and decorated.

Trammel A metal device with links or openings used in a fireplace for suspending pots or kettles at various heights over the flames.

Tramp art Chipped carving (notched) on layers of wood from cigar boxes. A simple tool such as a pocket knife was used and objects were often fashioned by itinerant laborers, not hobos.

Treen Comes from the word tree. Treenware is small wooden objects.

Trencher Wooden plate used for eating.

Trivet Fireplace stand for pots, pans, or kettles.

Whale oil lamps A lamp that burns whale oil.

Windsor chair American Windsors have backs with many slender spindles and splayed (slanting out) legs, which distinguish them from the English Windsors with their more vertical legs.

Wrought iron Can be shaped by pounding and fused by welding.

Index

About the Authors

When Bob and Harriett Swedberg research and write books, they travel thousands of miles. They meet many fine people who share their interest in preserving heritage articles for future generations. While they enjoy visiting museums, they do not include museum pieces in their books. The Swedbergs photograph only articles that are actually available to the public to purchase or are in the possession of people who have secured them to preserve and collect. To date, this couple has written books on oak, country furniture, wicker, Victorian, and advertising, as well as on refinishing and repairing antiques. They are available as speakers and enjoy teaching about America's heritage through antiques classes.